The major challenge in creating the Vietnamese Marine Corps was not in devising its organization but in inculcating its personnel with the attitudes and values unique to our Corps. This was all the more difficult because of many cultural differences that separated us. That an amalgam of Vietnamese river force and commando units would evolve into a division-size Marine Corps, repeatedly committed to battle in crisis situations as a major component of Vietnam's strategic reserve, attests to the valor of the Vietnamese and the dedication of their U.S. Marine Corps advisors.

Victor J. Croizat
Colonel, USMC (Ret.)

TURNER PUBLISHING COMPANY
412 Broadway • P.O. Box 3101
Paducah, Kentucky 42002-3101
(270) 443-0121

Turner Publishing Company Staff:
Randy Baumgardner, Editor

Library of Congress Control No. 00-112277
ISBN: 1-56311-663-4

Printed in the United States of America.
Additional copies may be purchased directly
from the publisher. Limited Edition.

WARRIORS

OF THE SEA

WARRIORS
OF THE SEA

Marines of the Second Indochina War

SEA TIGERS

Elite Vietnamese Marines and
their American Advisors
Compiled, Written and Edited by
Command Sergeant Major Michael Martin

TURNER PUBLISHING COMPANY
PADUCAH, KENTUCKY

Victor J. Croizat

Warriors of the Sea is dedicated to Victor J. Croizat, Colonel, U.S.M.C. (Retired)—Marine, historian, military diplomat, and the first American Advisor to the Vietnamese Marine Corps—and to the memory of General Le Nguyen Khang; also, to the heroic Vietnamese Marines who exemplified the true meaning of "above and beyond the call of duty."

ACKNOWLEDGEMENTS

Every Marine who served with the Vietnamese Marine—Thuy Quan Luc Chien—contributed in one way or another to this book; it is impossible to identify each by name or photograph, but we have attempted to capture the pride, professionalism and valor of the Vietnamese Marines and their American Advisors, and too, their honored place in military history.

Marines who rendered their time, photographs, and assistance to this effort were: Lieutenant General Anthony Lukeman, Victor J. Croizat, John W. Ripley, Thomas E. Campbell, Gerry Turley, Don Price, John Miller, Robert H. Whitlow, John E. Greenwood, Bruce Mellon, Jim Breckinridge, LeRoy V. Corbett, Gordon Keiser, Michael J. Gott, Cy Kammeier, Curtis G. Arnold, Charles D. Melson, Jack Shulimson, Charles M. Johnson, BGen Tran Van Nhut, Ton That Soan, Loung Nguyen, Tran Thien Hieu, and to Dr. Tran Xuan Dung for permission to use articles from the Vietnamese Marine Division book.

Others who provided individual support: Mike Tucker, Jim Waters, Bobby Jackson, Mrs. Nguyen Van The, Dai Le Duy, Johannes "Minn" Lee, Tam Chi Duong, Dang Van Thanh, Van Quang Truong, and Dr. Nicholas T.B. Dang.

A significant contribution in both text and photographs was made by Charles D. Melson, branch head/chief historian, Marine Corps Historical Center. He is an author and has written several books on the U.S. Marines. For his support and encouragement, he has my grateful gratitude.

I am indebted to Colonel Frank C. Foster (USA retired), President Of Medals Of America, WWW.USMEDALS.COM for the use of the Vietnamese ribbon chart; Marine and friend Douglas L. Humer, and Clement V. Kelly Jr. for the original flags, uniforms, patches, and insignia used in the color section of this book—as in my other books, they have provided tangible items of value that reflect the images of these elite units; and for his most generous and helpful information on insignia, Cecil B. Smyth has our thanks; his publications cover all Vietnamese units.

Institutions, associations and publications which provided support and are due our thanks are: National Archives, the Naval Academy, the history and museums Division of Marine Corps headquarters (Marine Corps series of chronological histories of involvement in Vietnam), Marine Corps Gazette, Leatherneck Magazine, Proceedings Naval Institute, Naval Review; the Marine Corps Association and the National Association of the Vietnamese Marine Veterans. Photographs provided by individual Marines or sources listed, and ECPA (photo cinéma video des armees).

Finally, with deep devotion to my lifelong companion and wife Hildegard Martin, who has shared the hardships and the joys of military service and my sojourn from private to Command Sergeant Major; her journey began at birth in war-torn Europe, with her father in a Soviet prisoner of war camp and her mother with children to rear among the rubble. She, as could most military spouses, write her own place in history.

PREFACE

Mike Martin

No one who's ever had anything to do with Vietnam came away entirely unchanged; including the American Advisors, especially the Marine Advisors (Co Vans). This former French colony—**colonie de la France**—that from its birth had fought for its independence from foreign dominance, would cast its spell of almost hypnotic power over many of these hardened warriors...they would become profoundly changed by their experiences, even those who were old "China-hands".

A country of unsurpassed beauty and passive tranquillity that could explode into chaos and destruction without warning, Vietnam—unlike many nations of the Far East—was a land of vast extremes, intolerable to the faint-hearted.

The South Vietnamese people were clearly polarized into two segments, the rural and the urban; each with a way of life and attitudes entirely different from the other. This, with the opposing civilian elements–ethnic minorities, political parties, students, religion and the culture–would confront both the audacious and tenacious performance of the Marine Co Van and his "charge of duties". His example on the battlefield and within the society itself would exemplify the professionalism of a combat leader.

Vietnam's Oriental mystique and color was not wholly hidden under the guise of war that it was subjected to. For the Co Vans, theirs was an opportune glance as a window into the unchanged East open—an exotic munificence from an older Orient: bronze-skin monks with unwaveringly dark eyes; gongs echoing across open rice paddies against a backdrop of carnelian sunsets; sparkling stars invading the privacy of secluded hamlets, peering through openings of dense forest canopies where menacing shadows dart and distort from hanging lanterns and flickering candles ... morning sounds—first crowing of game cocks and bare feet on winding paths, sounds of market vendors and school children with polished faces and bubbling gaiety, carrying their books in uniform fashion anticipating the joy of the days' venture.

Always, the pungent smells of culinary delicacies tantalizing the palate...charcoal and wood smoke that would intermingle with herbs, spices and nu'o'c mam, momentarily hung suspended, then swirling blended with evening breezes, creating a veil of intrigue in darkened passageways...marshy smells of heavy and damp atmosphere, warm rains in the afternoon and chilly nights in the highlands...stately over-arching trees along prosperous boulevards lined with colonial villas and greenish lakes dotted with garish pagodas; and the perpetual profusion of floral beauty (chrysanthemums, gladiolas, hibiscus, roses, poppies and orchids) that assaulted the eyes…much that would be obliterated by the harsh reality of war for the "Sea Tigers" and their Advisors—like the autumn mist of a thousand tears falling, theirs would be the melancholy memories of intimate death in combat against an elusive foe: each trail a source of mines and ambushes, each mountain crest a possible bunker complex, each tree lined canal presented the fearful frontal assaults, and the fresh crimson blood of slain comrades that seeped into the earth—the time eternal, spiritual bonding with warriors past and present.

The "sea-wave" camouflage and green beret identified the Sea Tigers, but their courage and fighting ability in battle earned them the title of "Marine," these descendants from the **Troupes Coloniales**—the French Marines—and the river assault groups (Dinassauts) of the First Indochina War.

Like the ancient crusaders who bore their cross marked shields across the Holy Lands, the U.S. Marine Advisor carried the coveted Corps symbol—Globe and Anchor—as an individual throughout Vietnam, adding to its lineage of loyalty, brotherhood, and honor—The Few and the Proud!

Vietnamese Marines are inserted for a ground sweep in the Mekong Delta. This amphibious operation was conducted to ferret out the Viet Cong guerrilla bases in this previously inaccessible area of swamps and bottomless mud. Note the M60 machine gun in the bow of the boat and the armored vests worn by the individuals.

INTRODUCTION

Colonel John W. Ripley

I cannot tell you with any degree of accuracy just how many advisors served with the Vietnamese Marines during the advisory period, and the following Vietnam War; probably 200 to 300. What is verifiably true, however, is that all of us, to a man, were greatly honored with this duty; and even further, most of us mark it as a defining moment in our lives; giving us all a great sense of accomplishment, professionalism, and most especially, pride.

From the very beginning, the Marines did things differently. We trained our Vietnamese counterparts here at our formal schools, and even their Drill Instructors were given a dose of our boot camp so that they could insofar as possible replicate it for their own Vietnamese recruits. It was not unusual for us to know, or know by reputation, the Commanding Officers of various battalions before we even arrived. Conversely, it was not unusual for the RVN officers to know us, and to ask for the services of a particular advisor. All of this of course had the effect of giving mutual confidence to the Vietnamese and the American Marines serving in the same Corps.

Recognizing the above, it was still common practice for the battalion commander—the "Counterpart" to the Marine Advisor as he was called––to put the new advisor through a few paces before accepting him, and certainly his advice, on any matters of fighting the battalion. Generally this had to do with observing him during firefights and other enemy actions, asking what he might have done in certain cases, and getting feedback from his subordinate company commanders on their feelings of the advisor's overall performance. Even if all of this was positive, the Vietnamese nature was to be cautious until their advisor had proven beyond any doubt that he was equal to their trust; especially as they averaged ten times the combat experience we American Marines came with, and all of us came with a considerable amount by Marine Corps standards.

The Vietnamese knew us advisors as "Co Van's"; a very proud term that roughly translates to "trusted friend". Interestingly, only Marine Advisors were called this. I never heard it applied to any other American, and no subsequent histories of the war refer to Co Vans, other than in reference to Marines. There were other Marine Advisors who were attached to Vietnamese Army units to include Rangers, Hoc Bao, even Airborne units for short periods, but especially the 1st ARVN Division, which operated exclusively around U.S. Marine battalions in I Corps; the northern-most provinces controlled by the 1st Marine Amphibious Force. Even these Marines were not referred to as Co Van for some reason.

There was still one other very major difference in the Marine Advisor and his battalion, and all other units advised by Americans. There were generally two advisors assigned to a battalion, but often-just one was present. In 1972 that became just one assigned, and at Dong Ha during the Easter Offensive, I was there by myself. No matter how many there were, however, the advisors remained in the field constantly with their battalion, and virtually side by side with their battalion commander counterpart. We were physically rarely separated so that conversations, radio transmissions, enemy actions, etc. could be seen, heard and commented on by both parties without misinterpretation. We shared the same food—literally––on many occasions eating from the same rice bowl, the same fighting hole, fears, hopes, disappointments, foul weather (often), and the exhilaration of triumph watching your Marines perform well as they did so often. You also shared the same dangers brought about by enemy action and the typical rugged life in the field. But as we could all see, the payoff was enormous. The level of confidence, and acceptance, we enjoyed by our Vietnamese Marines made it all worthwhile; miserable conditions and enemy action notwithstanding. We did not have an advisors hut or separate compound to disappear to, and thereby to enjoy the American perks that would filter their way out to us occasionally. Every night I dug my fighting hole next to my counterpart. Every night—even when we were inside the protection of a base camp—we were next to each other, asleep or awake, but always in view of our Marines. Advisors never commanded, but it was important to be seen as an authority figure, a symbol of command. In truth, there were numerous occasions when subordinates would look to you for the equivalent of commands; instructions, guidance, direction, all of which they interpreted as commands and acted accordingly. In my case I always made certain that my counterpart knew what I was saying, and as stated he was in most cases standing next to me, so that my guidance, instructions or "advice" had the effect of coming from him. Of the numerous enemy actions we fought, I took great pride in the fact that not once was I ever questioned, nor did anyone ever hesitate in following my suggestions.

In late March, early April of 1972 the Vietnamese Marines were put to the test as no other Vietnamese, or American, units had been throughout the then 12 year war. The enemy attacked across the DMZ in the Easter Offensive; the largest invasion since the Chinese crossed the Yalu River into North Korea in 1950, 22 years earlier—20,000 invaders in 14 divisions, over 200 tanks and 3 regiments of artillery, including the most significant weapon on the battlefield for them; SAM missiles. These would permit them to shut down our greatest advantage —air power—that is exactly what happened. The South Vietnamese nation was singularly fortunate that two brigades of Marines were there in the north along the DMZ, with the last brigade soon to follow. For the first time in their history the Vietnamese Marine Division would fight as a Marine Division, commanded by the Marine Commandant, their division commander, and what a difference they made. When all other units around them melted away in the furious enemy assault, and one surrendered, the Marine Division held. And not only did they hold, against what was estimated at the time to be 10-1 odds, which later turned out to be closer to 20-1 odds; they went into the attack! The price of course was enormous. In my battalion alone, stuck at Dong Ha which became the spearpoint of the enemy attack, we fought and bled our way from 735 Marines fit for duty when we arrived to less than 200 when we left, and on arrival in Hue City a month later exactly 52 stood in morning formation saluting our Commandant, a former 3rd Battalion Commander who came to pay us tribute.

All the Marine battalions suffered greatly, but fought and held their ground in the greatest traditions of elite warriors, which they were. Their battle ferocity was legendary as I witnessed over and over. They had nowhere near the supporting arms American units take for granted, indeed demand, and yet this never deterred them from taking the fight to the enemy. Their field skills were amazing considering they were not supplied with packaged rations or even fuel to cook what they were given. Imagine moving to contact along a mountain trail above Khe Sanh and in the rucksack of the Marine in front of you is a duck stuffed into one of the cargo pockets, his beak tied shut and looking back at you; undoubtedly knowing that he will be tonight's dinner—and a damn good one. Toward the end of the month when the "fresh rations" ran out we lived off the land––weeds, bulbs, roots, jungle animals, and God knows what. Advisors would on occasion get violently sick, but you were so important to the battalion that the Bac Xi (doctor, or surgeon) would immediately find a cure. Figuratively, or literally, he always had something up his sleeve. My assistant advisor on a dark night got himself snake bitten and immediately went into deliriums. We were on a mountain top deep into enemy territory trying to rescue a recon patrol. Evacuation was out of the question. Our Bac Xi went to his side after an hour of threading his way through the enemy between our perimeters, and by morning had revived him, stabilized him, and back to duty three days later. I could not help but reflect at the time that they would never have hazarded the loss of the only doctor in the field for even their own —to include the C.O.—under the circumstances.

A final observation burned into my memory is the extraordinary compassion the Marines had for their own civilians: refugees and non-combatants. Although they fought like furies from hell, when a non-combatant was hurt, or in trouble, they went to amazing lengths to remove them and protect them from the battle. It was a remarkable sight. These men had their own families at home. There is no question that seeing the suffering of the refugees greatly troubled them. In a shocking moment, my counterpart had a deserter removed from a truck loaded with booty he had obviously stolen from refugees, and in the presence of everyone had him executed while the unfortunate wretch begged and cried for compassion. The firing party put so many rounds through him that they knocked out the truck; a secondary misfortune, as we could have used it.

Another remarkable result of the Marine's reputation was demonstrated over and over on the battlefield when we captured the enemy, almost always in a severely wounded state. Because our "tiger stripe" uniforms were so unique and identifiable, the enemy knew we were Marines. Never happy to be captured, they nevertheless knew they would be treated with compassion and dignity. I never once saw otherwise. Underlying this feeling of mutual respect is an incident that took place in our 5th Battalion when a patrol was overrun resulting in the capture of 15 Marines. The enemy, knowing of the treatment their own POW's got, removed the weapons, watches, bootlaces, and other valuable equipment, and then released them. According to their Advisor, they even stated that they knew that they were Marines, and that they would not mistreat them.

A sad reality of the war, which was fought for another three years after we left, is that the elite units—Airborne, Rangers and Marines—where the loyalties and fighting skills were greatest, also suffered the greatest. Accordingly, few of them made their way out and eventually to the United States when the final curtain fell. For those who did we embraced them and looked after them in every way we could. Many have prospered, and our friendships have even grown. For those who entered the "reeducation camps" we know that their lives were pure hell; a contradiction of the battlefield esteem the enemy held in Marines. But of course, the political officers that ran the camps were nowhere near as experienced as the combat veterans where respect for their opponent would have been common.

For those of us whose lives were touched—changed forever—by the great tragedy of Vietnam, our memories are intense. Certainly, that is the case with me. I will go to my grave with the memory of Marines surrounding me at Dong Ha after I had destroyed the bridge. I had briefly collapsed, my head was swimming, and I was semi-coherent. They were stroking my face and my bare arms, not pulling or gripping, and saying in their melodious tone "Cam On Dui-Uy, Cam On Dui-Uy, VC Bien Chet, Het Roi". "Thank you Captain, Thank you. The Enemy is Now Gone, Dead—Unable to Get to Us. There are literally hundreds of more stories I could tell: poignant, brutal, exciting, and each of them hard to believe. The central element of each of these stories, however, is the extraordinary pride we all felt in serving with this great organization of Vietnamese Marines—unlimited, unexcelled PRIDE. We shall not see the likes of them again, but their reputation is eternal.

Then-Capt. John W. Ripley, the sole American Advisor to the 3d VNCM during the battle for Dong Ha on Easter Sunday 1972.

Final assault on Quang Tri City – September 11, 1972, Vietnamese Marines fight their way to the top of the Citadel's wall; by 1700 hrs on 15 September, the Marines had gained complete control of the Citadel. The VNMC had suffered 3,658 casualties in the seven-week battle.

THERE IS NOTHING AS FINE ON THE FACE OF THE EARTH AS A GOOD MARINE...

– GENERAL "CHESTY" PULLER

The Vietnamese Marine Commander, Gen. Le Nguyen Khang, addresses a formation of Marines at the Vietnamese Marine Corps Headquarters in Saigon. He wears the distinctive "sea-wave" camouflage uniform without service or unit insignia and the green beret.

Lieutenant General Le Nguyen Khang was the first and longest Commandant of the Vietnamese Marines (1960-1975). After completing the officer training school in '51, he served with the commando units from which the marines were formed in '54. He was a graduate of AWS (Amphibious Warfare School). These are his comments to the U.S. Marines in 1966 as a Major General.

VIETNAMESE MARINE BRIGADE—1966

General Le Nguyen Khang

As the United States Marine Corps reflects on 191 years of glorious history, in which it has distinguished itself in many ways, the Vietnamese Marine Corps is celebrating its 12th birthday. The Vietnamese Marine Brigade has been acknowledged as South Vietnam's finest fighting force, and we are proud of this distinction. But we are equally proud to be known as Marines and to be associated in spirit and in deed with the select group of professional military men of many nations who call themselves Marines.

The Marine brigade of 1966, a poised, professional and competent unit with numerous battle honors in its combat against Viet Cong and NVA forces, bears little resemblance to the organization which came into being by Presidential decree on 1 October 1954, as a separate component force of the Vietnamese Navy. As originally constituted, the brigade comprised several river groups or boat companies, and a number of ranger companies.

These forces resembled a French Dinassault or river assault group and were formed from the various commando units trained under the French. This composition was entirely in keeping with the mission assigned the Marine brigade, which was the maintenance of security on rivers and canals with the added responsibility of conducting limited amphibious operations on rivers and coast, if necessary.

From an initial activation strength of 1,137 officers and men, the brigade expanded steadily and by early 1955 included 1,837 Marines in a modified USMC organization of two infantry battalions and a Headquarters and Service Company. This organization gave the brigade additional maneuver elements and greater firepower as well as a limited capability to support logistically the tactical deployments of the battalions. By 1959, the brigade had added a Headquarters element and a third landing battalion within its framework of 2,276 Marines. The 4.2" mortar company provided principal supporting fires.

During all this period, the Vietnamese Marine Brigade continued to resemble the U.S. Marine Corps more and more in weapons, tactics, and structure. The big change in the brigade's organization, however, was effected in 1960 and 1961, as the brigade added a medical company, a 75mm pack howitzer battery, and another infantry battalion. The combat support and combat service support units were grouped into an Amphibious Support Battalion in 1962, the same year that the brigade added 105mm howitzers to its armament and an artillery battalion to its organization.

This basic organizational structure remains the same today. At the present time the brigade comprised five operational infantry battalions, an artillery battalion with one battery of 75mm pack howitzers and two 105mm howitzer batteries, and an Amphibious Support Battalion, which includes a Headquarters and Service Company, Landing Support Company, Signal Company, Medical Company, Reconnaissance Company, and a Military Police detachment, and its own training center. And as the brigade observes its 12th anniversary, now a separate service under its own command, a sixth infantry battalion is being activated and will soon take its place in the field with the other five infantry battalions, all of which have won battle honors.

That, briefly, is a chronological record of the brigade's steady progress through its 12 years of existence. The organizational changes and strength increases parallel and reflect the changes in the nature of the conflict in Vietnam and the increased effort by the armed forces of the Republic of Vietnam and the Free World. Keeping pace with the rising strength of the brigade, the command structure has been adjusted and revised to meet the requirements for control of more and larger battalions.

The inherent mission of the Vietnamese Marine Brigade, "to conduct amphibious operations to assist in the counterinsurgency effort" remains much the same. However, as part of the General Reserve Forces of the Republic of Vietnam, the brigade has been committed on order of the Joint General Staff to independent or joint ground operations in all four corps Tactical Zones of the country, usually in response to various critical situations, both political and military. As a force in readiness, the brigade's adaptability and mobility are attested to by the numerous major troop movements, which have been executed, usually on short notice, by land, sea, and air. The missions assigned have covered the entire spectrum of counterguerrilla operations: search and destroy, search and clear, reaction to contact, helicopter assault, static defense of a tactical area, and road security.

Until the formation of a Fifth Battalion in 1964, the brigade was usually employed piece-meal—or a single battalion at a time. With five battalions, however, the brigade became capable of retraining one battalion while fielding two task forces of two battalions each, with controlling task force headquarters, organic artillery support, and limited combat service support. The addition of the Sixth Battalion gives added versatility in that the brigade can now deploy two task forces of two or three battalions each simultaneously. Battalions not deployed are freed for security missions, local operations, or retraining.

Prior to 1965, most of the brigade's commitments were to the II, III or IV Corps Tactical Zones for extended ground operations. However, the Marine brigade managed to retain its amphibious capability by a number of operations in the Delta area, which were actually more riverborne assaults than amphibious operations. These were conducted from "Dong Nai" boats, the 14-foot Styrofoam and laminated fiberglass boats, which can operate close to riverbanks in about two feet of water. The "Dong Nai" boat, powered by a long-shafted 40 hp outboard motor, can carry nine fully combat equipped Marines at speeds up to 10 knots and is organic to the Transportation Company of the brigade. On one instance in 1964, though, the brigade made one amphibious operation utilizing fishing junks, each of which carried about 60 combat equipped Marines. Fire support ashore was provided by 75mm pack howitzers, which were dismantled into transportable components and then reassembled on shore.

During the years 1962-1964, the brigade began to fashion the combat record, which has led to its acceptance as one of South Vietnam's finest fighting forces. In 1962, the four battalions then in being were engaged in combat operations or in security missions in actively hostile areas about 32 percent of their time. By 1963, the percentage of combat operational time had risen to 59 percent; and in 1964, the four battalions were committed to operations about 83 percent of the time. And during that time, the Marines managed to kill Viet Cong at the rate of about five VC to every one Marine killed in action. The combat commitments and the kill ratio have continued at the same high percentages through 1965, and up to the present.

In 1965, the brigade was committed increasingly to the I and II CTZ; and during the spring of 1965, two battalions under the command of a task force headquarters, remained in II Corps near Bong Son in Binh Dinh Province for nearly four months. The Viet Cong paid for that deployment, as the Marines killed 444 and captured another 150. For their conduct during that campaign, and especially for the battle at An Thai Hamlet on 7-8 April, the 2nd Battalion of the Vietnamese Marine Brigade was cited by the Republic of Vietnam and was recommended for the Presidential Unit Citation by the United States.

In that battle, the 2nd Battalion, in defensive positions around An Thai, was taken under attack by a numerically superior Viet Cong force. The 2nd Battalion repulsed six different assaults in a nightlong battle fought entirely with organic infantry weapons. With superb fire discipline and leadership, each small unit of the 2nd Battalion held its ground and fought as a team. When overrun and by-passed by enemy forces, the Marines turned in their foxholes and shot down attackers from the other direction. After being slowly pushed

General Khang and an USMC Advisor visiting the battlefield near Bong Son, 1965. Note the bodies of the Viet Cong killed during the engagement.

back at dawn in a crushing seventh attack, the Marine forces rallied and counter-attacked to regain their positions and force the withdrawal of the Viet Cong. When the battle subsided, 205 enemy dead littered the battlefield—and 59 of the bodies were within the 2nd Battalion's perimeter.

This victory had special significance in the war because it clearly demonstrated to our allies that a trained, disciplined Vietnamese unit with determination and leadership, could defeat hard-core Viet Cong units of superior numbers. The victory was also an inspiring and stimulating page in our young history.

Although we have been teamed with United States Marine units in many operations since, our first cooperative venture with our brother Marines came in *Operation Blue Marlin* in November 1965. In that operation, the 3rd Battalion of the VNMB, made an amphibious landing north of Chu Lai in Marine LVTs from U.S. Navy LSTs, a richly rewarding experience. Every unit we encountered made us feel as true members of the "Marine Brotherhood," an added dividend to the amphibious experience we acquired in the operation. That operation set the stage for what we sincerely hope is mutual trust and respect between all Marine forces engaged in the fight against the Viet Cong in South Vietnam.

Since that time we have conducted two other amphibious operations in the Rung Sat Special Zone southeast of Saigon. The first operation utilized a Vietnamese Navy LST and gunships to land Marines to clear Viet Cong from along the Long Tao River; the second operation was *Jack Stay* in April of this year. In this operation, two Marine battalions participated with the Special Landing Force (1/5) of the 7th Fleet in a joint operation. The 5th Vietnamese Marine Battalion made a riverborne assault from Vietnamese Navy LCMs, while the 4th VNMB landed from helicopters to act as a blocking force for 1/5 and the 5th Battalion.

Many of our operations during 1966, have been in I Corps in conjunction with ARVN and United States Marine units, and we have continued our enviable record. There have been several memorable battles during the first months of this year, which have equaled An Thai in intensity and in number of forces involved. In April in the Quang Ngai area, the 1st Battalion—reacting rapidly to intelligence offered by a Viet Cong captive—made a sudden helicopter assault into the immediate vicinity of a Viet Cong regimental command post and in a fierce, pitched battle of only an hour or so killed 150 VC. And on 21-23 June, in Quang Tri Province, Task Force Bravo with two battalions made contact with an enemy force and punished it as it withdrew. Then the Task Force abandoned the chase, made a swift helicopter-borne landing to block the escape of the Viet Cong unit, and in a two-battalion assault killed 173 VC and captured another 23.

The Marine brigade's latest victory came in Operation "Lien Ket 52/Colorado," which included the Fifth Marines of the 1st Marine Division, some 2nd ARVN Division units, and three battalions of Vietnamese Marines. The VNMB task force included its own direct support artillery and a reconnaissance unit for pre-H-Hour security in the landing zone. The three battalions landed by helicopter on 6 August deep in the interior of Quang Tin Province, in three days killed 203 VC, and scored an overwhelming victory over an identified enemy regiment.

Then, still in contact with withdrawing remnants of one regiment, the task force on 13 August encountered another VC regiment in fortified, dug-in positions about 20 kilometers northwest of Tam Ky. The merit of the power-packed three-battalion task force became evident in the ensuing sharp, bitter struggle in which the Marines held off attacking enemy forces on one flank while making a determined assault on the main enemy positions to the front. Tactical aircraft and artillery coordinated by task force headquarters assisted the attack. The enemy force once again fled, leaving the battlefield littered with nearly 150 bodies. The final score reported by Vietnamese forces in this nine-day operation was 504 killed and 75 captured.

Operation "Lien Ket" proved once more that Marine units have the leadership and the firepower to meet a Viet Cong force of similar or greater strength in a head-on clash. The battle also confirmed that the Marine brigade concept of deploying a task force of adequate size, together with the required direct support artillery, reconnaissance units, engineers, and logistical support units, would return big dividends. It is our intention that Marine units continue with supporting elements.

Of course, no account of the Vietnamese Marine Corps would be complete without acknowledging the many contributions of the Advisors from the U.S. Marine Corps who serve with us. Their dedication to duty, valor, and sacrifices have been an inspiration to the Vietnamese Marines. Their service is indicative of the strong bonds of friendship that exist between the VNMC and the USMC.

We look to the USMC as a constant example of the finest in Marine traditions and we take great pride in the fact that many of our own officers have received training in USMC schools. I remember with pleasure my days in the Amphibious Warfare School, as does my Chief of Staff, Colonel B.T. Lann. Most of our battalion commanders are graduates of the AWS, and others will attend when possible. Many of our younger officers have graduated from the Basic School, and ten others are currently enrolled in the present class. And the influence of USMC schools extends through those enlisted Marines who are graduates of the Drill Instructor school in San Diego.

To the United Stated Marines, on behalf of the Vietnamese Marine Brigade, I offer my sincerest congratulations on your 191st anniversary. Be assured of our respect and admiration. We pledge that we will strive always to uphold our honor as Marines and to build within the Vietnamese Marine Corps those traditions and the *esprit de corps* that mark Marines everywhere!

Snapshot of Defeat: Marine commando provides security as Viet Minh prisoners are escorted out of a village.

DINASSAUT – MARINE COMMANDOS

The forerunner of the Vietnamese Marine Corps was the French Division Navale d'Assaut, Marine Nationale. On 10 April 1953, the first unit of the Vietnamese Navy, still with French cadres but under its own flag, was activated; this was the Can Tho Dinassaut (naval assault division). In June, the Vinh Long Dinassaut was activated. The Dinassauts were rivercraft units created by the French for the support of coastal combat operations and landbase garrisons along the Indochinese rivers. Dr. Bernard B. Fall stated, "Probably the bloodies river battles since the American Civil War were fought out between the French (Dinassauts) and the Viet Minh. A Dinassaut was composed of roughly twelve ships and two companies of Marine Commandos – formerly army commandos. Although these forces fought with great valor and success, the French concept of a Vietnamese Marine Corps did not extend beyond light assault-infantry type-units for riverine warfare. The Vietnamese Marine Corps was almost wholly a creation of the U.S. Advisory effort, but as of 20 August 1955, when the Vietnamese Naval Forces came under Vietnamese command, the formation and implementation of the Marines was mostly a Vietnamese decision.

Tonkin: Marine Commandos de la Dinassaut nr. 3, fighting in the midst of a village in ruins. French commando is armed with a submachine gun, "Pistolet Mitrailleur Hotchkiss 9mm;" the Vietnamese has a Mauser 98 bolt action rifle.

Commandos of Dinassaut nr. 3, make their way through flooded fields. Lead man has an Enfield caliber 303 rifle with grenade launcher.

Unmindful of the difficult terrain, the belligerent stares of these French-led commandos – most likely from one of the various ethnic groups – attests to their willingness to fight. The evening meal is hanging on the bamboo pole carried by two of the commandos.

ORIGIN OF THE VIETNAM MARINES

Colonel Victor J. Croizat, USMC (Ret)

The author's principal and self-assigned task in the confusing days following the end of the Indochina War, was to ensure that the infant Vietnamese Marine Corps would survive as an operational entity during the period of reorganization of the Vietnamese armed forces occasioned by the departure of the French and our assumption of "support" responsibilities. He has written the following summary of the origins of the Vietnamese Marine Corps.

By the end of 1949, the French had succeeded in creating a government in Saigon under Emperor Bao Dai to serve as the counter to the dissident government of Ho Chi Minh. The stage was thus set for the signing of the Franco-Vietnamese Agreement on 30 December 1949 providing for the establishment of separate Vietnamese Armed Forces, which were to include naval forces whose cadres, organizations, and training were to be provided by the French Navy.

There then ensued periods of inter and intra service differences in French military circles, which introduced long delays in the implementation of the Agreement. First, the French Navy had to resist the dominant French Army desire to have the Vietnamese Navy serve as a simple support element for the Vietnamese Army. Then, within the French Navy, the Saigon view that the Vietnamese Navy should begin as a "river navy" had to be reconciled with the Paris view that the Vietnamese should have an immediate "blue water" capability. As a consequence, it was not until 10 April 1953 that the first unit of the Vietnamese Navy, with French cadres but under its own national flag, was activated. This unit was the Cantho naval assault division; a river force organization whose activation indicated that the Saigon view regarding the importance of the river forces had prevailed.

The French experience in river warfare had revealed the necessity of integrating infantry elements with the afloat forces. These elements were at first provided directly from the Army. However, in time they acquired a special status and were variously designated river companies, light support companies, and commandos. The emphasis placed by the French upon river forces thus assured the continued existence of these specialized units, which were to serve as the forerunners of the Vietnamese Marine Corps.

The French Naval Command in Saigon had previously made reference to the desirability of organizing a Vietnamese Marine Corps. Moreover, the Franco–Vietnamese High Committee in its meeting of 15 February 1954 had gone so far as proposing that Vietnamese Marine Corps personnel man river patrol and the Dinassault craft as well as being formed into commandos and one "amphibious battalion." The existence of a Vietnamese Marine Corps was not, however, officially recognized until 13 October 1954 when Premier Ngo Dinh Diem signed the required decree. This document identified the origins of the Corps and established its mission and basic structure as follows:

"ARTICLE 1. Effective 1 October 1954 there is created within the Naval Establishment a corps of infantry specializing in the surveillance of waterways and amphibious operations on coast and rivers, to be designated as: "THE MARINE CORPS."

"ARTICLE 3. The Marine Corps shall consist of various type units suited to their functions and either already existing in the Army or Naval forces or to be created in accordance with the development plan for the armed forces.

"ARTICLE 4. These units will be of the following types.

River Companies

Landing Battalion

Light Support Companies

Commando

Naval Assault Divisions

The formal establishment of the Vietnamese Marine Corps suggests that the future of the corps was thenceforth assured. This, unfortunately, was not the case, for the United States support, agreement for the Vietnamese armed forces was at a substantially lower level than the strength of those forces in 1954. Thus, there followed a prolonged "numbers game" where each service sought to minimize the size of the personnel cuts it would have to take. This was particularly serious for the Naval Forces since the Vietnamese military establishment functioned under a single general staff and had a single budget. Thus, the Vietnamese Navy with something like 1/200 of the strength of the Vietnamese armed forces had little weight in inner council deliberations...when it was invited to attend them at all. By the same token, the Marine Corps, dependent upon the

Navy, was in the most unfavorable position of all. A measure of the criticality of this situation may be found in the fact that the initial plan for the reorganization of the Vietnamese Naval forces provided for a reduction of the Marine Corps from the 2,373 man strength that existed on 31 December 1954 to 1,000 men; this being the largest cut proposed for any service.

As events were to prove, the year 1955 was largely a struggle for the survival of the Vietnamese Marine Corps. That it did survive may be attributed to two basic accomplishments. The first was the reorganization of the Corps into a headquarters and two battalions. This was intended to bring together the varied units organized under the French whose worth was unquestioned but whose compositions were alien to U.S. concepts and whose modest size made them particularly vulnerable to force reductions. The second was the acceptance by the Chief of the General Staff of the need for a viable amphibious force capable of conducting offensive operations in river and coastal environments, and of serving with the Army's parachute regiment as the nation's general reserve. These accomplishments were given recognition on 7 December 1955 when Lieutenant General Le Van Ty approved the Naval Forces Reorganization Plan that called for a Marine Corps of 1,835 officers and men organized as indicated above, and further accepted in principle the Naval Forces Development Plan that called for the expansion of the Marine Corps into a three battalion force by 1959.

Operation "Barbe" 4-6 December 1950: Commandos de la Dinassaut nr. 3, assemble prior to embarkment aboard the Landing Craft Infantry (LCI). Note beret on French Commando and the crossed anchors patch of fleet personnel on the sleeve of one individual; patch is worn only on the left sleeve.

In retrospect, these accomplishments appear modest. However, when it is recalled that much of the Vietnamese Marine Corps was engaged in combat operations in the Mekong delta during 1955 and that the government itself was threatened by the Binh Xuyen insurrection in April of that year, the atmosphere of the period can scarcely be said to have been conducive to the orderly and progressive transition of a military establishment created under French concepts to one representing American and Vietnamese viewpoints.

Marine Commandos disembark as a contingent of the Dinassaut flotilla. Note the armored cannon turrets for direct fire support.

Making a commo check (requesting confirmation of transmission) with units of the 6 Dinassaut battalion that have deployed to construct an outpost at Hiep Tran, 3-10 May 1951.

Cochinchina – Operation "Jeanne d'Arc" 3-10 May 1951: 1er REC Regiment Etranger de Cavalerie, equipped with the Weasel MC29 ("crabes") and a battalion of French-Vietnamese Dinassaut nr.6.

The Geneva Agreement of July 1954, resulted in the partition of Vietnam and the creation of North and South Vietnam. Here, Vietnamese refugees leaving the North are aided by French sailors; they are loading them on a U.S. transport ship that will take them on their voyage on the South China Sea.

THE FORMATIVE YEARS

Marine Robert H. Whitlow

Military Assistance Advisory Group, Vietnam

When the Geneva cease-fire went into effect in the late summer of 1954, the machinery for implementing the military phase of the American assistance program for South Vietnam already existed. President Truman had ordered the establishment of a U.S. Military Assistance Advisory Group (USMAAG or MAAG) in French Indochina in mid-1950 as one of several reactions to the North Korean invasion of the Republic of Korea. Established to provide a material support to the French Expeditionary Corps, the MAAG constituted little more than a logistical funnel through which U.S. military aid had been poured.

Lieutenant General John M. "Iron Mike" O'Daniel, U.S. Army, had been assigned to command the MAAG in the spring of 1954. O'Daniel's selection for the Saigon post anticipated a more active U.S. role in training of the Vietnamese National Army. He had been chosen for the assignment largely on the basis of his successful role in creating and supervising the training programs, which had transformed the South Korean Army into an effective fighting force during the Korean War. Now, in the aftermath of the Geneva settlement, he and his 342-man group began preparing for the immense task of rebuilding South Vietnam's armed forces.

The entire American project to assist the South Vietnamese in the construction of a viable state was delayed during the fall of 1954 while the necessary diplomatic agreements were negotiated among American, French and South Vietnamese officials. President Eisenhower dispatched General J. Lawton Collins, U.S. Army (Retired), to Saigon in November to complete the details of the triangular arrangements. Collins carried with him the broad powers which would be required to expedite the negotiations.

By mid-January 1955, the president's special envoy had paved the way for the transfer of responsibility for training, equipping, and advising the Vietnamese National Army from the French to the USMAAG. He and General Paul Ely, the officer appointed by the Paris government to oversee the French withdrawal from Indochina, had initiated a *Minute of Understanding*. In accordance with this document, the United States agreed to provide financial assistance to the French military in Vietnam in exchange for two important concessions. First, the French pledged to conduct a gradual military withdrawal from South Vietnam in order to prevent the development of a military vacuum, which might precipitate a North Vietnamese invasion. Secondly, they accepted an American plan to assist in a transition stage during which the responsibility for rebuilding the Vietnamese military could be transferred to the MAAG in an orderly fashion. General Collins, in addition to engineering the understanding with General Ely, had advised Premier Diem to reduce his 210,000–man military and naval forces to a level of 100,000, a figure which the U.S. State Department felt the United States could realistically support and train.

The American plan to begin assisting South Vietnam encountered further delay even after the Ely-Collins understanding had been reached. Ely's government, arguing that the United States had agreed to provide only one–third of the amount France had requested to finance its Indochina forces, refused to ratify the agreement. The deadlock was finally resolved on 11 February 1955 when French officials accepted the terms of the Ely–Collins arrangement in a revised form.

A combined Franco-American training command, designated the Training Relations Instruction Mission (TRIM), became operational in Saigon the day following the French ratification of the Ely-Collins understanding. (The combined training mission originally was designated the Allied Training Operations Mission. This designation was changed prior to the time the mission became operational.) Headed by Lieutenant General O'Daniel but under the "overall authority" of General Ely, TRIM was structured to prevent domination by either French or Americans. The training mission was composed of four divisions, Army, Navy, Air Force, and National Security, each of which was headed alternately by either an American or a French officer. The chief of each division had as his deputy an officer of the opposite nationality. U.S. officers, however, headed the divisions considered by MAAG officials as the most important—Army and National Security. Operating through TRIM and assisted by the French military, the USMAAG was tasked with implementing the U.S. Military Assistance Program in a manner that would help shape the Vietnamese national forces into a cohesive defense establishment prior to the withdrawal of French forces.

Origins Of U.S. Marine Assistance

Only one U.S. Marine was serving with the USMAAG in Saigon when TRIM became operational—Lieutenant Colonel Victor J. Croizat (Other Marines, however, were present in Saigon at the time. They were those assigned to the American Embassy. One officer was serving as assistant naval attache for Air, and 12 other Marines were serving as security guards). Croizat's assignment to the U.S. advisory group had resulted when General Lemuel C. Shepherd Jr., Commandant of the Marine Corps, nominated him to fill a newly created billet as liaison officer between the

MAAG and the French High Command during the latter stages of the Indochina War. Largely because of his French language fluency and his former association with many French officers while attending their war college in 1949, Croizat was chosen for the assignment.

Lieutenant Colonel Croizat, however, did not arrive in Vietnam until 2 August 1954. By then, the cease-fire agreement had been signed at Geneva and the need for a liaison officer with the French High Command no longer existed. General O'Daniel, therefore, assigned the newly arrived Marine officer to serve on the General Commission for Refugees, which had been created by the South Vietnamese Government immediately after the cease-fire. In this capacity Croizat became directly involved in the construction of refugee reception centers and the selection and development of resettlement areas in the South. When U.S. naval forces began assisting in the evacuation of North Vietnam, Lieutenant Colonel Croizat was sent to Haiphong, the principal seaport of Tonkin. There he headed the MAAG detachment and was responsible for coordinating U.S. operations in the area with those of the French and Vietnamese. When the so-called "Passage to Freedom" concluded in May 1955, 807,000 people, 469,000 tons of equipment and supplies, and 23,000 vehicles had been evacuated from Communist North Vietnam (The French moved 497,000 tons of equipment and supplies, and 15,000 vehicles. The U.S. Navy moved the balance). It was not until February 1955 that the Marine returned to Saigon.

During Lieutenant Colonel Croizat's absence, Premier Diem had acted on a long-standing proposal to create a small Vietnamese Marine Corps. The issue of a separate Marine force composed of Vietnamese national troops had surfaced frequently since the birth of the Vietnamese Navy in the early 1950s. Although the proposal had been heartily endorsed by a number of senior French Navy officers, the downward spiral of the French war effort had intervened to prevent the subject from being advanced beyond a conceptual stage. Largely as a result of earlier discussions with Croizat, Premier Diem acted on the matter on 13 0ctober when he signed a decree which included the following articles:

ARTICLE 1. Effective 1 October 1954 there is created within the Naval Establishment a corps of infantry specializing in the surveillance of waterways and amphibious operations on the coast and rivers, to be designated as: The Marine Corps

ARTICLE 3. The Marine Corps shall consist of various type units suited to their functions and either already existing in the Army or Naval forces or to be created in accordance with the development plan for the armed forces.

In accordance with this decree, a miscellaneous collection of commando-type units was transferred from the Vietnamese National Army and Navy to the Marine Corps. Except for a naval commando unit, which had conducted amphibious raids along the coastal plains, these forces had operated in the Red River Delta with the French and Vietnamese Navy Dinassauts (river assault divisions). First employed in 1946, the Dinassauts had evolved into relatively effective naval commands capable of landing light infantry companies along Indochina's tangled riverbanks. Normally the Dinassauts was composed of about a dozen armored and armed landing craft, patrol boats, and command vessels. An Army commando unit, consisting of approximately 100 men, would be attached to such naval commands for specific operations. Thus organized, the Dinassauts could transport light infantry units into otherwise inaccessible areas and support landings with heavy caliber automatic weapons and mortar fire. Such operations had been particularly successful in the sprawling Red River Delta of Tonkin where navigable estuaries and Viet Minh abounded. (Of the dinassaut Bernard Fall wrote: "It may well have been one of the few worthwhile contributions of the Indochina War to military knowledge." Fall, *Street Without Joy*, p. 39. A more thorough analysis of dinassaut operations is included in Croizat, *A Translation From The French Lessons of the War*, pp. 348-351.) Later in the war, as the concept was refined, the French created a number of Vietnamese National Army commando units for specific service with the Dinassauts. Still attached to the Navy commands these units were sometimes responsible for security around the dinassaut bases when not involved in pre-planned operations. A number of these rather elite Vietnamese units, variously designated light support companies, river boat companies, and commandos, were now transferred to the newly decreed Vietnamese Marine Corps (VNMC).

By the time Lieutenant Colonel Croizat returned to Saigon in early 1955, these units, which totaled approximately 2,400 officers and men, had been evacuated from North Vietnam. Several of the commandos had been assembled at Nha Trang on South Vietnam's central coast where the French still maintained an extensive naval training facility. There, under the supervision of a junior French commando officer, several former commandos had been organized into the 1st Marine Landing Battalion (or 1st Landing Battalion). The balance of the newly designated Marine units, however, were scattered in small, widely separated garrisons from Hue to the Mekong Delta. These units included six riverboat companies, five combat support light companies, and a small training flotilla. Diem had appointed a former Vietnamese National Army officer, Major Le Quang Trong, as senior Marine Officer. But because no formal headquarters had been created and because no real command structure existed, Major Trong remained relatively isolated from his far-flung Marine infantry units.

Upon returning to Saigon, Croizat was assigned to the MAAG's Naval Section and subsequently to TRIM's Naval Division as the senior U.S. advisor to the newly created Vietnamese Marine Corps. In this capacity, the Marine officer quickly determined that the small Vietnamese amphibious force was faced with several serious problems. First, and perhaps its most critical, was that despite Premier Diem's decree, the Marine Corps continued to exist essentially on an informal basis. "The Marine Corps itself had no real identity," it's U.S. advisor later explained. "It was a scattering of dissimilar units extending from Hue to the Mekong Delta area." The fact that its widespread units were still dependent on the French Expeditionary Corps for logistical support underscored the weakness inherent in the VNMC's initial status.

Other problems arose from the continuation of French officers in command billets throughout the Vietnamese naval forces. Under the Franco-American agreement, which had created TRIM, a French Navy captain doubled as chief of the combined training missions, Naval Division and as commanding officer of the Vietnamese naval forces. This placed the French in a position to review any proposals advanced by the U.S. Marine advisor. Complicating the situation even further, a French Army captain, Jean Louis Delayen, actually commanded the 1st Landing Battalion at Nha Trang. (Delayen, described by Croizat as "an exceptionally qualified French Commando officer," later attended the USMC Amphibious Warfare School at Quantico.)

Demobilization presented another potential difficulty for the Vietnamese Marine Corps in early 1955. Under the U.S.-Vietnamese force level agreements, the Vietnamese naval forces were limited to 3,000 men. The Marine Corps, which alone totaled a disproportionate 2,400 men, had been instructed to reduce its strength to 1,137 men and officers. With no effective centralized command structure and so many widely separated units, even the relatively simple task of mustering out troops assumed the dimensions of a complex administrative undertaking.

In short, the very existence of the Vietnamese Marine Corps was threatened in a number of interrelated situations. The continuation of a separate and distinct Marine Corps hinged ultimately, of course, on the overall reorganization of the Vietnamese armed forces and their support structure. Essentially, it would be necessary to establish a requirement for such an organization within South Vietnam's future military-naval structure. Croizat personally sensed that this would be the pivotal issue in determining the VNMC's future. "There were numerous representatives of the three military services from each of the three countries concerned with the fate of the Vietnamese Army, Navy, and Air Force," he pointed out. "But, there was no champion from within the Vietnamese Marine Corps since no Corps existed except on paper." Thus, it was left initially to a French captain, a Vietnamese major, and a U.S. Marine lieutenant colonel to keep alive the idea that South Vietnam's defense establishment needed a separate Marine Corps.

Political Stabilization And Its Effects

During early 1955, the entire South Vietnamese government was engulfed by a crisis, which threatened to disrupt the American plans to help build a viable anti-Communist country. The crisis occurred not in the form of an overt North Vietnamese attack but rather as a result of the South's political instability. In February, the leaders of the Hoa Hao, the Cao Dai, and the Binh Xuyen, dissatisfied with Premier Diem's refusal to accede to their various demands, formed the United Front of National Forces.

By mid-March the disaffected leaders of these organizations felt strong enough to test the premier's strength. Trouble began late that month when the Hoa Hao began undertaking guerrilla type activities against Diem's National Army units in the sect's stronghold southwest of Saigon. On 28 March, Diem ordered a company of paratroops to seize the Saigon Central Police Headquarters that the French had allowed the Binh Xuyen to control. Fighting erupted throughout the capital the next day as Binh Xuyen units clashed with loyal government forces. A truce was arranged finally in the city on 31 March after three days of intermittent but fierce fighting. That same day, the Cao Dai broke with the United Front and accepted a government offer to integrate some of its troops into the National Army.

An uneasy peace prevailed over South Vietnam until 28 April when new fighting broke out. By the middle of May, government forces had driven the Binh Xuyen forces from Saigon, fracturing their organization. Remnants of the bandit group, however, escaped into the extensive Rung Sat swamps south of the capital where they continued fighting individually and in small groups. In the countryside south of Saigon, 30 of Diem's battalions, including the 1st Landing Battalion, took the offensive against the Hoa Hao regular and guerrilla forces.

The national crisis, for all practical purposes, ended in the last week of June when a Hoa Hao leader surrendered 8,000 regulars and ordered his followers to cease all anti-government activities. Sporadic fighting continued, however, as Diem's forces sought to mop-up Hoa Hao splinter groups fighting in the western Mekong Delta and Binh Xuyen elements still resisting in the rugged mangrove swamps south of the capital. In August the Marine Landing Battalion fought a decisive action against the remaining Hoa Hao in Kien Giang Province about 120 miles southwest of Saigon, destroying the rebel headquarters. Later in the year, the 1st Landing Battalion, joined by several riverboat companies, reduced one of the last pockets of Binh Xuyen resistance in the Rung Sat. As a result of these and similar actions being fought simultaneously by loyal Army units, organized resistance to Premier Diem gradually collapsed. (Some sources contend that remnants of the Hoa Hao and Cao Dai armies survived to operate alongside the Viet Cong guerrillas who began threatening the Diem government in the late 1950s. Kahin and Lewis, *The U.S. in Vietnam*, p. 111.)

The sect crisis of 1955 proved to be the turning point in Diem's political fortunes. At the height of the crisis, Emperor Bao Dai attempted to remove Diem as premier by ordering him to France for "consultations." Electing to remain in Saigon and direct his government efforts to quell the

Lieutenant Colonel Victor J. Croizat, first U.S. Marine Advisor to the Vietnamese Marine Corps, translates during discussions between Lieutenant General John "Iron Mike" O'Daniel, USA, Chief, USMAAG, Vietnam, and Premier Ngo Dinh Diem.

rebellion, the Premier declined Bao Dai's summons. The Vietnamese military forces proved loyal to the Premier, having faithfully executed Diem's commands throughout the emergency. Having successfully met the armed challenge of the sects and the Binh Xuyen and having openly repudiated Bao Dai's authority, Premier Diem had imposed at least a measure of political stability on South Vietnam.

An epilogue to the sect crisis was written on 23 October when a nationwide referendum was held in South Vietnam to settle the issue of national leadership. In the balloting, since criticized as having been rigged, Premier Diem received 98.2 percent of the total vote against Bao Dai. Three days later, on 26 October, South Vietnam's new president proclaimed the Republic of Vietnam (RVN).

The Vietnamese Marine Corps benefited greatly from Premier Diem's successful confrontation with his political rivals. On 1 May, in preparation for the 1st Landing Battalion's deployment to combat, Major Trong had established a small Marine Corps headquarters in Saigon. Shortly thereafter, Diem had appointed a Vietnamese officer, Captain Bui Pho Chi, to replace Captain Delayen as commander of the landing battalion. The French commando officer, who was a member of TRIM, remained at Nha Trang as an advisor to the VNMC. Then, on the last day of June, Diem removed the remaining French officers from command positions throughout South Vietnam's naval forces. The combined effect of these actions was to reduce French influence throughout the nation's naval establishment while making the Vietnamese Marine Corps more responsive to the central government.

The burdens of demobilization also were lightened somewhat as a result of the sect crisis when a new force level was approved by the United States in mid-summer of 1955. The new agreement, dictated in part by the requirement to integrate portions of the sects' armies into the national forces, raised the force level to 150,000 men and placed the personnel ceiling of the Vietnamese naval forces at 4,000 men. This revision enhanced the prospects for a corresponding increase in the authorized strength of the VNMC.

The 1st Landing Battalion's performance against the sect forces in the Mekong Delta and the Rung Sat, moreover, tempered much of the previous opposition to a separate VNMC. Heretofore, U.S. and Vietnamese Army officers had opposed the existence of a Vietnamese amphibious force apart from the National Army. Until the sect uprising, Lieutenant Colonel Croizat had used the influence afforded by his position as naval advisor to the general staff to advocate the continuation of the VNMC. But during the sect battles, the Vietnamese Marines had firmly established their value to the new government. By displaying loyalty, discipline, and efficiency in combat, they had spoken out in their own behalf at a critical juncture in their corp's existence.

Shortly before the 1st Landing Battalion deployed to fight the rebellious sect forces, two additional U.S. Marine advisors—an officer and a noncommissioned officer—arrived in South Vietnam for duty with the MAAG. Both Marines were assigned to TRIM. Croizat dispatched the officer, Captain James T. Breckinridge, to Nha Trang where he soon replaced Captain Delayen as advisor to the 1st Landing Battalion. As State Department policy prohibited U.S. military personnel from participating in combat activities with indigenous forces, Breckinridge was forced to await the battalion's return from the field. During its absence, he divided his time between Nha Trang and Saigon where he assisted Colonel Croizat with planning and logistics matters. The noncommissioned officer, Technical Sergeant Jackson E. Tracy, initially remained in Saigon, but later moved to Nha Trang. There, serving principally a small unit tactics instructor to the Vietnamese Marines, Tracy impressed Breckinridge as a "first-rate Marine 'NCO'—one who could carry out the most complex assignment with little or no supervision."

Soon after 1956 opened, President Diem appointed a new officer to head the Vietnamese Marine Corps. On 18 January, Major Phan Van Lieu assumed command of the VNMC, and thereby became the second senior Marine Officer.

Reorganization And Progress

The 1st Landing Battalion remained in action against the Binh Xuyen remnants until February 1956. During this period, Lieutenant Colonel Croizat reviewed the entire organizational structure of the Vietnamese Marine Corps. By now the size of the service had been reduced to roughly 1,800 officers and men although it retained its original organization of six river boat companies, five light support companies, a landing battalion, a training flotilla, and a small headquarters.

This organization, with so many dissimilar units existing on one echelon, influenced Croizat to suggest that Major Lieu restructure the service. Assisted by Croizat, Captain Breckinridge, and Technical Sergeant Tracy, Lieu and his small staff spent several months developing and refining plans for the comprehensive reorganization of the Marine Corps. Lieu submitted this package to the Vietnamese Joint General Staff (JGS) on 21 December 1955. The salient feature of the plan was to create an additional landing battalion without increasing the 1,837-man ceiling which then governed the size of the VNMC. Significantly, the plan contained a clause proposing that the Vietnamese Marine Corps, be expanded to regimental size in the future.

The Vietnamese Joint General Staff approved the new structure, and reorganization of the VNMC was begun when the 1st Landing Battalion finally returned to Nha Trang in February. The old riverboat and light support companies were disbanded and three new units—a 4.2-inch mortar company, a headquarters and service company, and a new landing battalion—were formed. Designated the 2nd Landing Battalion, this new unit formed about 25 miles south of Nha Trang at Cam Ranh Bay where the French had trained amphibious forces during the latter stages of the Indochina War.

While this reorganization was underway, Lieutenant Colonel Croizat initiated a search for acceptable means of expanding the Vietnamese Marine Corps to regimental size. A staff study produced by the senior Marine Advisor a month before the first phase of the reorganization effort had begun, included several important recommendations. Croizat proposed to General O'Daniel that authorization be granted to raise the ceiling on the VNMC from 1,837 to 2,435 officers and men. This, the Marine advisor pointed out, could be accomplished without affecting the overall ceiling on all South Vietnamese military and naval forces. By reassigning to the Vietnamese Marine Corps an amphibious battalion still organized within the National Army, the 150,000-man force level would not be altered. This would transform the Vietnamese Marine Corps into a three-battalion regiment and would unify all South Vietnamese amphibious forces under a single command. Croizat's study further recommended that the Vietnamese Marine Corps be designated part of the general reserve of the nation's armed forces and that it be controlled directly by the Vietnamese Joint General Staff. Although no immediate action was taken on these recommendations, they were to serve as a blueprint for the future expansion of the VNMC. Equally important, they bore the seed that would eventually make the Vietnamese Marine Corps a fully integrated component of South Vietnam's defense establishment.

During the ensuing three years, several apparently unrelated occurrences impacted either directly or indirectly on the U.S. Marine advisory effort in South Vietnam. The French completed their military withdrawal from South Vietnam and dissolved their High Command in April 1956, slightly ahead of schedule. (A few French naval officers and noncommissioned officers remained at Nha Trang as instructors until late May 1957.) In conjunction with this final phase of the French withdrawal, the Training Relations Instructions Mission was abolished. Thus, it was no longer necessary for the MAAG programs to be executed through the combined training mission.

Shortly after the departure of the last French troops, Lieutenant Colonel Croizat ended his assignment as Senior Marine Advisor. He was replaced by Lieutenant Colonel William N. Wilkes Jr., in June 1956. A veteran of the Guadalcanal campaign, Wilkes came to Vietnam from Washington, D.C. where he had recently completed a French language course. Like his predecessor, the new Senior Marine Advisor was scheduled to serve in Vietnam for two years.

In August, less than two months after Lieutenant Colonel Wilkes' arrival, President Diem appointed a new officer to head his Marine Corps. This time Bui Pho Chi, the captain who had commanded the 1st Landing Battalion during the sect uprising, was selected for the assignment. Chi's appointment was only temporary, however, for in October Diem ordered Major Le Nhu Hung to assume command of the Marine Corps. Major Hung, who became the VNMC's fourth senior officer, was to hold the position for four years.

An attempt to abolish the Vietnamese Marine Corps coincided with the series of changes in its leadership and the departure of Lieutenant Colonel Croizat. During the summer months, the Vietnamese Minister of Defense proposed that the VNMC be made a branch of South Vietnam's Army. Fortunately, the recent combat record of the 1st Landing Battalion outweighed the minister's influence and the effort to disestablish the Vietnamese Marine Corps was thwarted.

Another noteworthy incident in the record of the early relations between the U.S. and Vietnamese Marines occurred when the Marine noncommissioned officer billet within the MAAG was upgraded to an officer position. This adjustment, which anticipated the creation of the 2nd Landing Battalion, had the effect of making a U.S. Marine officer available to advise individual VNMC battalions on a permanent basis. Thus originated a plan whereby a U.S. Marine officer would advise each Vietnamese Marine battalion—a concept abandoned only temporarily between 1959 and 1962.

The Vietnamese Marine Corps continued as a two-battalion regiment under the command of Major Le Nhu Hung from mid-1956 through 1959. During this period Lieutenant Colonel Wilkes and his successor, Lieutenant Colonel Frank R. Wilkinson Jr., a Marine who had served as an aide to President Franklin D. Roosevelt, instituted a variety of programs intended to provide the Vietnamese Marines with a common base of experience and training. Perhaps the most important of these was one implemented in 1958 whereby Vietnamese Marine officers began attending basic and intermediate level schools at Marine Corps Schools, Quantico. The Vietnamese Marine Corps in South Vietnam established other formal schools for noncommissioned officers. In an effort to build *esprit de corps* among the lower ranking Vietnamese Marines, the U.S. advisors encouraged voluntary enlistment. They also persuaded their Vietnamese counterparts to adopt a corps-wide marksmanship-training program similar to the one then in use by the U.S. Marine Corps.

In conjunction with the reorganization of the VNMC and the stress being placed upon small unit and individual training, much of the U.S. advisory effort during this period was devoted to logistics. The Marine advisors soon discovered that the Vietnamese officers, who had not been directly concerned with supply matters under the French, tended to ignore this important area. "The real problem," explained Captain Breckinridge, "was the newness of it all. The Vietnamese officers simply possessed no base of experience or training in logistic matters." This shortcoming dictated that the American advisors not only design a workable logistics system but closely supervise its operation as well. Wilkes and Wilkinson instituted intensive schooling of supply and maintenance personnel and emphasized the value of command supervision to the Vietnamese leaders. The Marine advisors, for example, taught their counterparts that equipment shortages could often be prevented if command attention were given to requisitions. Still, even with constant supervision and formal schooling, the Vietnamese Marine Corps continued to experience problems in this area throughout the 1950s and well into the next decade. Breckinridge, who returned to serve with the Vietnamese Marines again as a lieutenant colonel in the late 1960s, recalled shortages of such vital and common items as small arms ammunition even then.

The years between 1955 and 1959 also saw the Marine advisors working to overcome a potentially more serious problem, one that also dated from the French-Indochina War. From the outset of their experience with the Vietnamese Marine Corps, the Marine advisors perceived that a strong defensive orientation seemed to pervade every echelon of the small service. Most Americans, including U.S. Army advisors who were encountering similar difficulties with the Vietnamese Army, agreed that this "defensive psychology" was a by-product of the long subordination of the Vietnamese National forces to the French High Command. Indeed, a criticism frequently voiced by USMAAG officials during the Indochina War had been that the French tended to frustrate the development of the Vietnamese military forces by assigning them static security tasks rather than offensive missions. Even though the forerunners of the Vietnamese Marine battalions had operated as commando units, they too had seen extensive duty protecting Dinassault bases and other French installations. Now this defensive thinking was affecting the attitude of the Vietnamese Marine toward training. Moreover, it was threatening the American effort to transform the service into an aggressive amphibious strike force.

By nature, this particular problem defied quick, simple solutions. The Marine advisors, therefore, undertook to adjust the orientation of the entire Vietnamese Marine Corps over a prolonged period through continuous emphasis on offensive training. The advisors consistently encouraged their Vietnamese counterparts to develop training schedules, which stressed patrolling, ambushing, fire and maneuver, and night movement. In this same connection, the Marine advisors translated U.S. Marine small unit tactics manuals into French, whereupon the same manuals were further translated by Vietnamese Marines into Vietnamese. This process assured that adequate training literature was made available to the individual Marine and his small unit leaders. The offensively oriented training programs and the translation project complemented one another, and combined with continuous supervision by the U.S. Advisors and the return of young Vietnamese officers from Quantico, gradually helped impart a more aggressive offensive spirit to the entire Marine Corps.

First group of Vietnamese Marine officers to attend U.S. Marine Officers Basic School, Quantico, Virginia, pose with Lieutenant Colonel Frank R. Wilkinson, Jr. (second from right), and Captain Michael Gott (extreme right). At the extreme left is Captain Le Nguyen Khang, a future Commandant of the Vietnamese Marine Corps. To his immediate left is Major Le Nhu Hung, a senior officer of the VNMC.

The Creation Of MACV And Marine Advisory Division

The American military build-up called for by the Washington decisions of December 1961 was well underway as the new year opened. Several U.S. units introduced in the closing weeks of 1961 had already begun operations by January. These included two U.S. Army transport helicopter companies and a composite U.S. Air Force detachment. Designated FARM GATE, composed initially of 151 officers, and men, the Air Force detachment had a dual mission of training VNAF elements and conducting attack sorties in support of President Diem's forces. The arrival of another U.S. Air Force unit, a C-123 transport squadron, another Army helicopter company, and an Army communications organization, the 3rd Radio Research Unit, just after the first of the year raised the number of American military personnel serving on permanent assignment in Vietnam to over 3,000. Assigned to the Army's radio unit, which immediately began operations from Pleiku in II Corps Tactical Zone, were 42 Marines from the 1st Radio Company, FMF. Designated Detachment A, 1st Radio Company, these were the first U.S. Marines to participate in the ongoing build-up.

Thus far, however, the U.S. troops arriving in Vietnam were for combat support rather than advisory type duty. At a meeting held in Honolulu in mid-January, Secretary of Defense McNamara ordered the ranking American military officials concerned with Vietnam to make substantial increases in the number of advisors serving with the Vietnamese armed forces.

Less than a month after the Honolulu conference, a new U.S. command was created in Saigon to manage the expected influx of advisors and the intensified military assistance effort more efficiently. On 8 February, the U.S. Military Assistance Command, Vietnam (USMACV or MACV) supplanted the MAAG as the senior American command in the Republic of Vietnam. Its commander, Army, General Paul D. Harkins (ComUSMACV), assumed direct responsibility for all U.S. military policy, operations, and assistance to President Diem's government. Harkins was directly subordinate to the Commander in Chief, Pacific, Admiral Harry D. Felt, whose headquarters was in Hawaii.

Under the new U.S. command arrangement, the old Military Assistance Advisory Group became subordinate to General Harkins' command. Headed by Major General Charles J. Timmes, U.S. Army, the MAAG was now responsible primarily for the advisory aspect of the assistance program. To accommodate the impending increases in the number of advisors, the MAAG's staff was restructured. Under its new table of organization, Marine Officers were to serve as deputy chief of staff and head of the plans branch of the J-3 division. Later, in 1963, the MAAG's table of distribution would be modified with the effect that the chief of staff billet would be held by a Marine colonel. The first Marine to serve as General Timmes' chief of staff would be Colonel Earl E. Anderson, a much-decorated aviator who eventually would become the Assistant Commandant of the Marine Corps.

The reorganization of the MAAG brought about a dramatic change in the size and scope of the U.S. Marine advisory effort. The new table of organization included a provision for an 18-man Marine Advisory Division within the MAAG's Naval Section. The organizational charts for this division included advisor billets for a lieutenant colonel, a major, six captains, a gunnery sergeant, and four staff sergeants. Administrative positions were to make up the balance of the new organization.

As had been the case previous to this expansion, the lieutenant colonel was to serve as the Senior Marine Advisor to the Vietnamese Marine Corps. The inclusion of the major's billet was expected to enhance the overall effectiveness of the advisory division as he was to double as Assistant Senior Advisor and as senior artillery advisor. The gunnery sergeant was to assist in the artillery advisory duties. Of the six captains, four were to be assigned as advisors to VNMC infantry battalions while the two others were slated to advise on engineer and supply matters. The four logistics-trained staff sergeants were to be assigned as assistant infantry battalion advisors and were expected to free the officer advisors from direct involvement in time-consuming supply matters.

Marines required to man this enlarged advisory unit began arriving in Vietnam as early as February. All of the new officer advisors were graduates of either Junior School at Marine Corps Schools, Quantico or the U.S. Army Special Warfare School at Fort Bragg, North Carolina. Following their assignments, but before departing for Vietnam, many advisors received schooling in military assistance operations. This normally included a five-month course of instruction in the French language, a requirement that more and more Marine advisors were beginning to question as a result of the Vietnamese desire to converse in their own language rather than French. Upon arrival in Saigon, the Marines were given two days of orientation briefings at MACV headquarters before assuming their jobs in the Marine Advisory Division.

Lieutenant Colonel Brown continued to serve as the Senior Marine Advisor and headed the new advisory division throughout the summer of 1962. In October, he was relieved by Lieutenant Colonel Clarence G. Moody Jr., a veteran who held the Navy Cross for heroism as a company commander during the Korean War. Having served with the British Royal Marines following Korea, Moody was somewhat familiar with the problems involved in dealing with foreign military services.

Encouraged by Brown and Moody, the U.S. Marine advisors participated in every combat operation undertaken by the VNMC during 1962. Prior to planned operations they helped their Vietnamese counterparts coordinate the more sophisticated means of support, which became available as the American military build-up took hold. During planning phases, for example, they assisted with the development of detailed orders and helped plan for employing artillery fire and air support. If the impending operation was to be amphibious in nature, the Marine officers coordinated with the U.S. Navy advisors assigned to the supporting Vietnamese Navy units, thereby insuring that planning for embarkation had been accomplished. On occasion, the advisors were required to coordinate helicopter support for the VNMC units—a task sometimes complicated by the Vietnamese Marines' lack of experience in heliborne operations. Unfortunately, the almost constant combat assignments being drawn by the handful of U.S. and VNAF helicopter units available in Vietnam made training in such operations impossible.

Even more difficult were the advisor's responsibilities after their units deployed to combat. The U.S. Marines were experiencing the often frustrating task of actually searching out the elusive Viet Cong on a continuing daily basis. Additionally, the Americans found themselves faced with the unenviable task of advising Vietnamese officers, who, in some cases, had been fighting Communist guerrillas since the French-Indochina War. These circumstances presented a unique set of challenges for the advisors. For American officers with relatively little actual experience in this brand of warfare to offer tactical advice in a form acceptable to their Vietnamese counterparts demanded a combination of tact, patience, and subtle persuasive powers.

The Advisory Division And VNMC Operations

At the beginning of 1963, the Marine Advisory Division, still headed by Lieutenant Colonel Moody, consisted of 8 Marine officers and 10 noncommissioned officers. In April, however, the table of organization was adjusted slightly when the First Sergeant and four assistant infantry advisor (noncommissioned officers) billets were eliminated. Another small unit training advisor was added to the organization, changing the strength of Lieutenant Colonel Moody's command to eight officers and six noncommissioned officers. Men from the 3rd Marine Division continued to augment the advisory effort and gain combat experience while serving in Vietnam on temporary assignments.

Like the U.S. organization, which advised and assisted it, the Vietnamese Marine Corps began the new year at the same strength that it had achieved when it had been expanded to brigade size in early 1962. Still commanded by Lieutenant Colonel Le Nguyen Khang, the Vietnamese Marine Brigade continued to operate as part of the nation's general reserve under the direct control of the Vietnamese Joint General Staff.

As the year opened three of the four VNMC infantry battalions were garrisoned separately in small, crude, self-sustaining camps around Thu Duc on the northern outskirts of Saigon. The 4th Battalion maintained its camp at Vung Tau on the coast. The newly formed artillery battalion, which became fully operational in mid-January when B and C Batteries passed their final gunnery examinations, was garrisoned near Thu Duc. While the Marine units spent little time in their base camps, being deployed almost continuously in combat, the Joint General Staff normally kept one battalion at Thu Duc, to enable it to respond to any emergency that might develop.

For the Vietnamese Marine Corps, 1963 was to be highlighted by innovations in the important areas of training and operations. Prior to Lieutenant Colonel Moody's arrival in Vietnam, all Vietnamese Marine recruits had received basic training at ARVN installations, an arrangement tolerated but never appreciated by the U.S. Marine advisors. Before his departure in the fall of 1963, Moody was able to convince Khang that he should push for the authority to establish a separate Marine training center. In late 1963, the JGS approved this proposal, whereupon the Vietnamese Marine engineers, advised by Captain Robert C. Jones, began building a small training facility at Thu Duc. In a related action Moody set in motion plans to have a small number of specially selected Vietnamese Marine noncommissioned officers sent to the Marine Corps Recruit Depot at San Diego for training as drill instructors. Although these plans would not come to fruition during Moody's assignment, the concept of a separate recruit-training center promised to permit the Vietnamese Marine Corps to establish and maintain its own.

Accomplishments

Even though 1963 closed upon a discouraging note, the Marine Advisory Division could report positively on its own activities. At the urging of the Senior Marine Advisor, the Vietnamese Marine Corps had reinstituted multi-battalion combat operations. Steps had also been taken to cut the VNMC's last formal ties to the ARVN by creating a separate Marine Corps recruit training facility. When activated this training center was expected to provide VNMC battalions with a stream of enlisted men who would possess a background of higher quality basic training.

As for personal achievements, the U.S. Marine Advisors had accompanied their units in every combat operation during 1963 except the November coup. No advisors had been killed in the 12-month period and only four (two of whom were on temporary assignment from the 3rd Marine Division) had been wounded. The first combat decorations other than Purple Heart medals for wounds were also approved and awarded to the advisors during the year. On 13 December, Captains Don Christensen and Frank Zimolzak, former advisors to the 4th and 3rd Battalions respectively, were awarded the Bronze Star Medals with the Combat "V" for meritorious service. Captain Richard Taylor, an advisor with the 2nd Battalion, earned the first Silver Star Medal during the same period for "conspicuous gallantry" between November 1962 and October 1963. Captain Joseph N. Smith, advisor to the 2nd and 4th VNMC battalions, earned the second Silver Star for gallantry displayed between October 1963 and April 1964. (Both Silver Star Medals were awarded during 1964.)

A Restructured Military Assistance Command

In many respects, 1964 was a year of transition for the U.S. Military Assistance Command, Vietnam. Not only did the command experience a change in leadership when General Westmoreland replaced General Harkins as ComUSMACV, but it was thoroughly reorganized in preparation for the more vigorous U.S. advisory program, which was expected to begin about midyear.

The major organizational change within MACV took place on 15 May when the MAAG was abolished and its staff integrated into that of the senior command. In June, MACV itself was restructured under a new table of distribution. These changes reflected the anticipated influx of advisors and support personnel, and therefore concerned the Army more than the other U.S. armed services.

Initially, the number of Marine billets on the restructured Military Assistance Command staff did not change substantially. Twenty-four Marines (15 officers and 9 enlisted) were included in the new table of distribution. This represented a net increase of only one over the number previously assigned to the MAAG and MACV staffs. By the end of September, however, Marines temporarily assigned to the MACV staff from FMFPac commands brought the on-board strength to 37. Another increase occurred in the early fall when eight more permanent Marine billets (three officers and five enlisted) were approved.

Changes In Marine Leadership

Two key links in the Marine Command chain that joined government policy decisions in Washington to Marine Corps operations in Vietnam changed hands during the first 60 days of 1964. On 1 January, General Wallace M. Greene Jr., replaced General Shoup as

Commandant of the Marine Corps. Greene, known in American military circles as a brilliant staff officer, had been serving since 1960 as Chief of Staff of the Marine Corps. By 1964, he had become an outspoken supporter of South Vietnam's struggle for independence. As a member of the Joint Chiefs of Staff and as a Chief of Service, his presence in administration policies would be felt until his tour as commandant ended on 31 January 1967.

An equally important change occurred in early March when General Greene named Lieutenant General Victor H. Krulak to replace General Roberts as Commanding General, FMFPac. A 1934 graduate of the U.S. Naval Academy, Krulak had won the Navy Cross during ground action in World War II. He arrived in the Pacific from Washington where he had served both Presidents Kennedy and Johnson as special assistant for counterinsurgency matters. Having made numerous fact-finding trips to Vietnam in this capacity, he was intimately familiar with the unique political-military struggle being waged there. He also had a reputation of being one of Washington's most vocal advocates of resisting communist aggression in Southeast Asia. A dynamic leader and a man of strong convictions, Krulak was to exert a pervasive influence over all Marine operations in the Pacific for nearly half a decade. Less obvious but of immense importance to both the Marine Corps and to the future of U.S. military operations in Vietnam was a change instituted within MACV by General Westmoreland during the early part of the year. The command's modified table of organization called for the establishment of a Deputy ComUSMACV billet to be filled by an Army general officer. The joint table of distribution for the reorganized command specified that an Army general would also fill the chief of staff billet—a position which had been held by General Weede since MACV's creation in early 1962. Thus, when Weede's assignment ended in May, Major General Richard G. Stilwell, U.S. Army, became Westmoreland's chief of staff while Lieutenant General John L. Throckmorton, U.S. Army, became Deputy ComUSMACV. (For his service as MACV chief of staff, General Weede was awarded the Distinguished Service Medal.) The Marine Corps, however, did not lose its entire senior presence on the MACV staff. Brigadier General Carl A. Youngdale, an officer whose 30-year career included distinguished combat tours in both World War II and Korea, arrived 15 January for assignment as Assistant Chief of Staff, J-2 (Intelligence). His presence on the MACV staff would insure a Marine voice in U.S. military planning at the Saigon level. Still, many Marines saw their relative strength on Westmoreland's staff seriously reduced—a change which seemed to mark somewhat of a turning point in the overall management of the military assistance effort.

Re-Designation And Reorganization

The reorganization of the U S. Military Assistance Command, Vietnam, had little initial effect on the Marine advisory program. With the dissolution of the MAAG, the old Naval Section, under which the Marine advisors had operated since 1955, was redesignated the Naval Advisory Group, MACV. Lieutenant Colonel Noren's Marine Advisory Division, whose authorized strength remained at 11 officers and 9 enlisted men through the first half of the year, was also renamed in mid-May. Known thereafter as the Marine Advisory Unit, Vietnam, the organization continued to function in much the same manner as it had under the previous arrangements.

The last five months of the year, however, saw some substantial changes in the composition of the Marine Advisory Unit as the advisor build-up recently approved by the Secretary of Defense began. Colonel William P. Nesbit, a recent graduate of the Naval War College in Newport, Rhode Island, relieved Colonel Noren (promoted from lieutenant colonel on 1 July) as the Senior Marine Advisor on 4 September. Colonel Nesbit arrived in time to supervise the implementation of a new table of organization, which added eight first lieutenants and a captain to the advisory unit in November. (A number of the Marines scheduled to fill the newly created billets did not arrive until early 1965.) The captain and one of the lieutenants were assigned as advisor and assistant advisor respectively to a new Vietnamese Marine infantry battalion, which was in the process of being formed. Four other first lieutenants joined Colonel Nesbit's command as assistant advisors to existing infantry battalions and one became the assistant artillery advisor. The two remaining lieutenants were assigned as advisors to the brigade's motor transport and communications companies, replacing noncommissioned advisors. Two billets were downgraded in rank: the engineer advisor from captain to first lieutenant, and the artillery advisor from major to captain.

In addition to phasing out three enlisted advisor billets, these changes relieved the Assistant Senior Marine Advisor of his artillery responsibilities. Colonel Earl E. Anderson, who had been serving since mid-1963 as the MAAG Chief of Staff, was instrumental in bringing about this particular modification. Under the old arrangement, the Senior Marine Advisor's presence frequently had been required at the MAAG headquarters in Saigon while the Vietnamese Marine Brigade headquarters was deployed to combat. As the Assistant Senior Marine Advisor was likewise torn between two jobs, Anderson had directed that he be relieved of artillery advisory duties. Thus, Major Raymond C. Damm, an officer who had served as Assistant Naval Attaché in Saigon between 1959 and 1961, became the first full-time Assistant Senior Marine Advisor after he joined Colonel Nesbit's command in May. When the changes were finally completed, the restructured and redesignated Marine Advisory Unit included permanent billets for 24 officers and men (18 officers and six enlisted men).

Another important aspect of the overall Marine advisory program was altered in the closing months of 1964. Since Lieutenant Colonel Croizat's tour with the Vietnamese Marines in the immediate post-Geneva period, most Marine advisors had attended French language courses prior to departing for service in Vietnam. As French influence in Vietnam faded during the late 1950s, however, the requirement for the language had gradually diminished, particularly as French maps were replaced by American ones. By the early 1960s, this situation had prompted several Marine advisors to recommend that instruction in French be replaced by Vietnamese language training. Primarily through the persistence of Colonels Moody and Noren, the policy was revised in 1964. The arrival of the new advisors in the fall marked the first time that Marine officers had received formal Vietnamese language training before beginning their tours. Colonel Nesbit, who had the advantage of commanding advisors trained in both languages, saw the change as "a marked step forward," in improving the advisory effort."

A Team Effort: Marines from the 7th Commo Battalion, 3rd U.S. Marine Division (Radio Relay Instruction Team), provide communications training to the Vietnamese Marines. Left to Right: Capt. Ramsey, Communications Advisor; LtCol Bao, VNMC Communications Officer; Maj. Than, Commanding Officer VNMC Signal Battalion; CWO Haughley, and members of his team.

A U.S. Marine Advisor inspects the weapons of a Vietnamese Marine unit; military skills, dress, bearing and courage, were traits required in setting the example for the Vietnamese.

Vietnamese Marines ride on a tank (M24) from an ARVN armor unit which could support an attack or provide fire support in the defense.

THE VIETNAMESE MARINE CORPS-VNMC
(THUY QUAN LUC CHIEN-TQLC)

Marine Charles D. Melson

The period following World War II saw a number of associated Marine Corps found in the Republic of China, the Republic of Korea, the Republic of Vietnam, the Philippines, Indonesia and Thailand. They had been formed, with the help of foreign military aid, to fight the various conflicts to contain Communist expansion in the region. Also present at various times were other Marines from the Netherlands, France and Great Britain. The beginnings of the Cold War witnessed this proliferation of amphibious forces in Asia, in part because of the reputation the U.S. Marines had earned in the cross Pacific drive against Japan and in other post war confrontations.

Three Corps fought together in Vietnam from 1965 through 1973. Each of these Corps were similar formations, but with its own history and traditions: the United States Marines, the Vietnamese Marines, and the Korean Marines. Common to each was a reputation for toughness on themselves and any foreign or domestic enemies; strong unit pride and loyalty; and a privileged place within the political structure of their respective countries. This is the story of one of them.

When the French departed Indochina in 1954, they left behind the fledgling armed forces of the Vietnamese Republic. Included were the riverine forces of the navy and an assortment of army commandos that had provided the troops for them. These had formed the river assault divisions (Dinassauts) that Dr. Bernard B. Fall observed as "one of a few worthwhile contributions" to military tactics of The First Indochina War (1945-1954). The commandos were formed into two battalions and grouped at Nha Trang when the separation of Vietnam into north and south was completed. After the Geneva Agreement that arranged the withdrawal of France from Indochina and the partition of Vietnam into north and south pending elections, the Americans moved to help the Government of South Vietnam against the Communist bloc supported People's Republic of Vietnam.

On 1 October 1954, the mixed commando units were designated as the Marine Infantry of the Vietnamese navy. In April 1956, it became known as the Vietnamese Marine Corps of the navy consisting of a Marine Group of two landing battalions. In 1961, the Vietnamese Marines became part of the South Vietnamese armed forces general reserve. Expansion resulted from successful employment against dissidents and bandits, which lead to the forming of a 5,000-man Marine brigade in 1962. Vietnamese Marine Corps influence increased in part with the role it played in complex national politics that saw Marines involved in coups in 1960, 1963 and 1964. This continual balancing of power was reflected in assignment of forces, commanders and the direction of the war.

The formation of its own training and replacement centers allowed the Marines to keep up to strength without relying on the army for manpower. Both officers and men attended schools in the United States at Quantico, Virginia, where a generation of Vietnamese and Americans met and served together. One Marine commandant, General Le Nguyen Khang, observed that his men were proud "to be associated in spirit and deed with the select group of professional military men of many nations who call themselves Marines".

Of the total of 565,350 South Vietnamese in the armed forces in 1965, more than 6,500 were Marines. This figure expanded to over 15,000 men in 1973. Total casualty figures are not available, but in the heavy 1972 fighting, some 2,455 Marines were killed in action and another 7,840 men were wounded during the same period. In 1965, the Vietnamese Marine Brigade was organized into a corps headquarters, two task force headquarters ("A" and "B"), five infantry battalions, an artillery battalion, and supporting units of engineers, motor transport, military police, medical, and reconnaissance. Headquarters were located in Saigon with outlying facilities at Song Than, Thu Duc and Vung Tau. A colonel, who was dual-hatted as a service and the brigade commander, commanded it. By this time, Vietnamese Marines were separated from the Vietnamese navy and answerable to the high command of the Republic of Vietnam Armed Forces. Present was a 28-man advisory unit from the American Marine Corps. American field advisors were down to the battalion level.

By 1966, the Marines formed another battalion and realigned supporting units to become a more balanced combined arms force. It was still lacking in armor, aircraft and logistic support. In 1968, a Marine Division was formed of two brigades. In 1970, there were three brigades, nine infantry battalions, and three artillery battalions. Supporting units continued to be formed through the following year, reaching a peak of 939 officers and 14,290 men at the time the Americans withdrew. To face the military crisis in 1975, three additional battalions and a fourth brigade were formed in time for the South Vietnamese defeat.

An examination of some of the corporeal aspects of the Vietnamese Marines is useful before considering their performance. This is the "soldier's load' in more than just material because it reflects the corporate tradition or myth. Specific designations and numbers existed to identify clothing and equipment were complicated by different languages, though in most cases, names were just the translation of the equivalent terms for, at first French, and then American items. There were also different designations for the same item: a generic term used by the Marines, the supply term used to catalog the item, and the manufacture's jargon. Generic nomenclature is used with the vernacular terms used by Marines to find a balance between regulation and reality for the decade covered.

The Vietnamese Marines used naval rank insignia with army rank titles. Eight enlisted grades existed and seven officer grades were used through sub-brigadier general (the one star grade). The rank structure reflected French influence, beginning with private, private first class, corporal, chief-corporal, sergeant, chief sergeant, adjutant, and chief-adjutant. Officers were the more conventional candidate through second lieutenant, first lieutenant, captain, major, lieutenant colonel, and colonel. Silver braid on black was worn instead of the naval gold. Officers and enlisted men both wore their rank on shoulder boards. In the field, this was simplified to wearing a single shoulder board on the front of the shirt. This resulted in a miniature version that could be fastened on a shirt or pocket button. By the end of the period, miniature rank insignia embroidered in black on green cloth was worn on the collar or headgear in the fashion of the Americans. All three types of rank badge were in use throughout the war. On occasion, Vietnamese army pin-on rank was worn during joint operations.

Distinctive organizational emblems evolved with the service over time and defy documentation. The earliest emblems included Vietnamese navy badges worn on caps and berets. These were in metal and embroidered forms. The emblems were gold for officers and silver for enlisted men. The distinct Marine Infantry badge had a much longer service life. It displayed crossed anchors surrounded by a plain circle. It was in both metal and embroidered variations. The embroidered beret badge used dark blue and then green backing. The officer's embroidered version had a wreath of rice stalks around crossed anchors central design; the enlisted version had only the crossed anchors.

In 1959, a new service device was adapted with an eagle, globe and anchor motif. It closely followed the American Marine emblem, but evolved to incorporate traditional Vietnamese features. According to an official document these included an anchor through a globe for the Marine's naval character, a five pointed red star with Vietnam in the center indicating combat spirit and the five parts of the world, and an eagle spreading its wings represented unyielding martial spirit. A black background stood for bravery in difficult situations - the color of a "death volunteer." This design eventually formed the basis for cap, beret, unit, and service insignia. Again, there were both officer and enlisted versions. The metal cap and beret badges were gold and silver for officers and brass for enlisted. The embroidered beret badge was backed in green and then later in red.

A Vietnamese Marine squad boards a US Army UH-1D helicopter for an air assault operation. Uniforms and equipment consists of ARVN packs, small arms, and M72 antitank rockets.

While initial field uniforms were unmarked similar to the American Marines, major variations of service and unit insignia developed. One Marine advisor recalled that in 1967 he wore the brigade shoulder patch, a service emblem on his pocket, and the colored battalion nametape. First used, was a full color service emblem on a black shield worn on the upper left sleeve indicating the Marine Group or Brigade. Later a full color service emblem on a green circle was worn on the right breast pocket as a corps insignia at about the time additional brigades were formed. Finally, a full color emblem on a green shield was worn on the upper left sleeve to indicate the Marine Division, replacing the previous brigade emblem. The emblem on the left sleeve was in line with the Army of the Republic of Vietnam practice. Cloth emblems worn on the combat uniform were generally of a high quality woven (Bevo) manufacture. Printed variations were for general service issue.

Battalion insignia developed at the same time from colored name tags worn over the right breast pocket that were based on colors used to assemble units after amphibious or riverine landings. Noted in use were the following colors: division or brigade headquarters units were green with white letters, the 1st Battalion in blue with white letters, 2nd Battalion in purple with black letters, 3rd Battalion in olive with white letters, 4th Battalion in red with black letters, 5th Battalion in maroon (black?) with gold letters, 6th Battalion in green with black letters, 7th Battalion in orange, 8th Battalion in blue with red letters, and 9th Battalion in brown with green letters. The artillery battalions used white and red combinations (1st Artillery Battalion used white with red letters), while the amphibious support battalion used green with gold or red letters. American advisors added a tape over the left breast pocket that had "U.S. Marines" in black on green, while their name tapes on the right were in white on green.

Eventually distinct battalion patches were worn on the upper right sleeve. The infantry battalions had a series of nicknames and slogans that were reflected on their battalion insignia: 1st Battalion's "Wild Bird," 2nd Battalion's "Crazy Buffalo," 3rd Battalion's "Sea Wolf," 4th Battalion's "Killer shark," 5th Battalion's "Black Dragon," 6th Battalion's "Sacred Bird," 7th Battalion's "Black Tiger," 8th Battalion's "Sea Eagle," and 9th Battalion's "Mighty Tiger." For the artillery units, this was the 1st Battalion's "Lightning Fire," 2nd Battalion' s "Sacred Arrow," and 3rd Battalion's "Sacred Bow." Support and service battalions followed this example, as well.

Uniforms were used on ceremonial occasion with the addition of white gloves, white duty belts, colored neck scarves, white parade shoulder cords, medals, ribbons, fourrageres, and white bootlaces. The Marine band had its own distinct variation on this theme that included a tailored uniform worn outside the trousers. Four classes of unit awards existed and were indicated by fourrageres worn on the left shoulder in red (gallantry), green (merit), yellow (national), and combination of all three colors for nine previous citations.

Like the other Marines, the Vietnamese had a series of uniforms that reflected climate and occasion: service dress with coat and tie, khaki dress, and combat dress that became its characteristic uniform as the war went on. A black navy beret and badge of the Marine Infantry were worn at first, but by 1965, standard headgear was a green beret with Marine Infantry badge. Also worn were a utility cover or rain hat in sea-wave camouflage pattern. The M1 helmet was used with either a net or American pattern cloth camouflage cover. The first combat uniform worn was the olive green shirt and trousers used by the army. This remained in use as basic training and fatigue clothing well after the adoption of the camouflage uniform, more from economy than sentiment. The sea-wave pattern uniform, or tiger stripes, was adopted in 1956 as a distinctive combat uniform. The four-color cloth was imported and manufactured into uniforms in South Vietnam. There were also examples of the army camouflage leaf pattern being used. This allowed for considerable variations in style and quality. In general, it consisted of a shirt with two covered chest pockets, trousers with two thigh and two seat pockets. Pen and cigarette pockets were popular modifications on the shirt sleeves and trouser legs. A black web belt with solid face brass buckle was issued. The American Marine open face buckle was popular as well. Footwear ranged from local Bata canvas jungle boots, full leather boots, to the American tropical combat boot.

The Marines that went to war in 1965 should have reflected knowledge of the "soldiers load," a subject that was examined critically by S.L.A. Marshall and the U.S. Marine Corps Schools early in the 1950's. In practice, considerations of culture, supply, and circumstance were shown to have been just as important factors in determining what was carried into battle. Individual combat equipment varied greatly over the period, from a mixture of French and American surplus to the standardized issue of M56 load carrying equipment from the U.S. Military Advisory Command Vietnam beginning in 1965. This included the replacement of M44 and M45 combat and cargo packs with the theater designed semi-rigid indigenous rucksack, the "ARVN pack." A distinctive Vietnamese field item was the individual hammock made from parachute nylon and suspension lines. In 1965, the Vietnamese were armed with American .30 caliber small arms that had been in existence since World War II; M1 rifles, M1 carbines, M1911 pistols, M1A1 submachine guns, and M1918 Browning automatic rifles. This required the use of webbing and accessories to carry the ammunition and magazines for these weapons. This was followed by outfitting with M16s and newer small arms by MACV at the same time as the other South Vietnamese forces. The Marines were a priority for this along with the airborne units of the national reserve. Another characteristic Vietnamese field item was the ever-present aluminum squad cooking pot. The cooking pot was an essential item in the way the Vietnamese fed in the field. The Marines carried five days of rations of rice, dried salted fish, and canned sardines.

Vietnamese Marines firing M29 81mm mortars; the mortars provided fire support at battalion level.

What was not issued had to be acquired locally. A typical meal consisted of five types of food: one salted, one fried or roasted, vegetable soup, green vegetables, and rice. A fermented sauce, nuoc-mam, was served as a spice and source of protein. Problems also resulted if the tactical situation prevented meals from being obtained and prepared. If circumstances did not allow resupply or preparation, then the Marines would go hungry. This included any American advisors that were present, most of whom lost weight with the Vietnamese in the field.

By 1960, the date on Vietnam's Campaign Medal, a state of armed conflict existed between the two Vietnams and their allies, The Second Indochina War (1960-1975). This was a civil war that had international connotations between several world powers and their clients. It was a confrontation that displayed a full spectrum of violence from individual terrorist acts and guerrilla fighting to conventional land combat, with extensive sea and air components. Enemy forces ranged from National Liberation Front guerrillas in South Vietnam of varying quality and quantity, to the regulars of the People's Army of Vietnam who were infiltrated into South Vietnam along the Ho Chi Minh Trail. They also defended North Vietnam with forces that were more conventional.

The Southeast Asia Theater of Operations was divided into North Vietnam, South Vietnam, the Tonkin Gulf littoral, and the inland frontiers of Laos and Cambodia. The country of South Vietnam consisted of political provinces grouped together into military regions or tactical zones numbered from I through IV, from north to the south. The country was divided geographically from east to west into a coastal plain, a piedmont region, and the central highlands.

As part of the national reserve, the Vietnamese Marines found itself from the 17th Parallel in the north to the islands of the extreme south. When assigned to a specific corps area, the Marines would serve under Army of the Republic of Vietnam (ARVN) general officers, the corps commanders. Prior to 1965, most operations were by single battalions in III and IV corps. A variety of counterinsurgency operations were engaged in, to include search and destroy, search and clear, helicopter and riverine assault and security tasks. Characteristic employment was in response to critical situations requiring rapid movement with short notice.

After 1965, the Marines deployed more to the II and I corps areas as the war progressed away from the Delta and Capital regions. Multiple battalion operations became the norm through the use of task force headquarters. Two battalions under Task Force "A" concluded a series of operations over a four-month period that resulted in 444 Communists killed and another 150 taken prisoner. This included a notable engagement in

April 1965 near An Thai, Binh Dinh Province, which resulted in the 2nd Infantry Battalion earning a U.S. Presidential Unit Citation for a successful defense against a superior communist force.

From 1966 through 1967, the Marines spent more time in I corps and conducted operations in conjunction with the Americans in this critical locale. It was observed that Marines were in the field 75% of the time, then the highest figure obtained by South Vietnamese forces. During the 1968 Tet Offensive, the Marines fought in both Saigon and Hue to defeat the Communist attempt at a general uprising. During this year, the Vietnamese Marines maintained a casualty to kill ratio of one to seven.

In March 1969, the 5th Infantry Battalion earned a U.S. Naval Unit Citation for action in III corps, near Bien Hoa. This resulted in 73 Communists killed, 20 taken prisoner and captured weapons. The Marines took part in the aggressive South Vietnamese external operations that coincided with the American departure: Cambodia in 1970 and Laos in 1971. The Laotian incursion was the first time a division command post took the field to control maneuver brigades.

By 1971, at least two Marine brigades remained in I Corps facing the demilitarized zone and the North Vietnamese. This filled, in part, the vacuum left when the Americans moved from this region. During the Spring Offensive in 1972, the Vietnamese Marines were fully employed for the defense of the north and at first were used piecemeal under control of the 3rd ARVN Division. The Marine Division established itself as a major fighting force in the month-long battle to recapture Quang Tri City. In the process, they killed an estimated 17,819 North Vietnam-

Then 1st Lt Chuck Melson USMC, in Military Region 1, South Vietnam. In 1972, he was with the 9th Marine Amphibious Brigade in direct support of the Vietnamese Marine Division and First Regional Advisory Command during the Easter Offensive.

ese soldiers, took 156 prisoners, and captured more than 5,000 weapons and vehicles. At the beginning of 1973, the Marine Division was regarded by the South Vietnamese as an "outstanding unit" of the Republic of Vietnam Armed Forces.

The Vietnamese Marines remained committed to the defense of the demilitarized zone through 1974. First ordered to protect Hue and Danang from the Communist attack in Spring 1975, the Marines were hastily withdrawn with the collapse of the South Vietnamese in the northern provinces. Five battalion commanders and some 40-company commanders were killed during the fighting. The division reorganized and deployed its remaining forces at Long Binh for the final battle for Saigon. There it stayed through the subsequent fighting at the end of April 1975. At that point, the Vietnamese Marine Corps ceased to exist except in memory and history. For the Vietnamese, the conflict was the end of a 30-year civil war in which the Vietnamese Marine Corps played a part until the bitter end.

Vietnamese Marine Corps Division Band, Saigon, at the dedication of the VNMC Marine War Memorial, 1971.

Major General Bui The Lan, Commandant of the Vietnamese Marine Corps, 1972-1975, reviews a unit's honor guard. Note the unit fourragére worn on the left shoulder; fourragéres represented four classes of unit awards.

THE VIETNAMESE MARINE CORPS

This article was written by **Cecil B. Smyth Jr.** *utilizing the following sources: Duong Tam Chi, Col. William E. Gro, Col. Turley, USMC, The Vietnam Experience and personal observations while in Vietnam.*

The Vietnamese Marines were a proud and well disciplined combat force, generally committed on short notice for independent or joint ground operations. They were the fire brigade of the RVNAF.

Originally formed as a group from seven companies of the French Riverine Force (Force Fluvial), the Headquarters and 1st Infantry Battalion were activated in August 1954, the 2nd Infantry Battalion in January 1955. In 1958 the 3rd Battalion was formed and in 1960 the 4th. Each battalion had a name, the 1st, Monster Bird (Quai Dieu), the 2nd, Crazy Buffalo (Tran Dien), the 3rd, Sea Wolf (Soi Bien) and the 4th, Killer Whale (Kinh Ngu).

In 1961, the Marine Brigade was formed consisting of the four infantry battalions, an artillery battalion and a company each of communications, engineers and transportation. The artillery was called Thunder Fire (Loi Hoa) and the four firing batteries were made up of two platoons of 75 mm howitzers and one platoon of 105 mm howitzers.

In 1963, the Marines were expanded into two brigades, A and B, and placed under the OPCON (operational control) of the Joint General Staff (JGS). A brigade had the 1st, 4th and 7th Battalions, the 7th being formed in 1966 and called the Gray Tiger (Hum Xam). The B Brigade had the 2nd, 3rd and 5th Battalions. The 5th was formed in 1964 and was called the Black Dragon (Hac Long). The 6th Battalion, called the Suicidal Sacred Falcon (Than Ung Cam Tu), was formed in 1965 and along with the artillery battalion, communications, engineer and transportation companies, were attached, as required, to either of the brigades.

On 1 October 1968, the Marine Division was formed. It originally consisted of the two brigades with supporting units. In 1970, a third brigade was added. The Division was organized as follows:

The 147th Brigade replaced the A Brigade: 1st, 4th, and 7th Battalions, 1st Artillery Battalion.

The 258th Brigade replaced the B Brigade: 2nd, 5th, and 8th Battalions, 2nd Artillery Battalion. The 8th Infantry Battalion was formed in 1969 and was named Sea Hawk (O Bien). The 2nd Artillery Battalion was also formed in 1969 and was named the Sacred Arrow (Than Tien).

The 369th Brigade, called the Royal Brigade, consisted of the 3rd, 6th and 9th Infantry battalions and the 3rd Artillery Battalion. The 9th Battalion was organized in 1969 and was called Strong Tiger (Manh Ho). The 3rd Artillery was formed in 1970. Its name was Sacred Bow (No Than).

The Division also had a Sea and Land Battalion, Engineer Battalion, Communications Battalion and a Medical Battalion.

In January 1975, the 468th Brigade was formed by taking one company from each of the nine battalions to provide the JGS an additional reserve. The brigade consisted of the 14th, 16th and 18th Infantry battalions and a 105 mm howitzer platoon.

The Marines participated in many combat actions during the more than 20 years they existed. Highlights follow:

On 28 December 1964, the VC occupied Binh Gia, a North Vietnamese resettlement village in Phuoc Tuy Province. The VC withdrew after two days of ARVN attacks. The 4th Marine Battalion participated in a sweep of the village with no contact, however, a U.S. Army helicopter was shot down and the four-man crew killed. Over half of the battalion became casualties in attempting to retrieve the bodies of the Americans.

In 1967, the 3rd and 4th Battalions operated with U.S. Task Force 117 in Operation Coronado II in the Mekong Delta. They landed right on top of a VC camp and killed 145 as they charged through the camp.

During the communist Tet offensive of 1968, the Marines were airlifted to Phu Bai where they joined the U.S. Marines and fought along side them to retake Hue.

Lam Son 719, the South Vietnamese invasion of Laos, began 8 February 1971, but the Marines did not get into action until 3 March when two brigades occupied fire support bases enabling the 1st ARVN Division to attack west to Tchepone. The 147th Brigade moved into FSB Delta and the 258th occupied FSB Hotel. During the withdrawal, the 147th was surrounded and subjected to intense artillery fire. On 21 March, the base was assaulted and was able to hold with the help of artillery, TAC air and a B-52 strike. More than 300 Marines were killed and wounded. The following day, running low on ammunition, the Marines withdrew as best they could, suffering heavy casualties. LTG Le Nguyen Khang, the Marine Commander, was very critical of the planning of Lam Son 719 from the beginning. His criticism seems justified as his Marines lost a brigade without having participated in any offensive action.

River assault boats recon by fire into enemy controlled areas, circa 1969. "Tango Boats" prep the beach at Mam Can in southern Mekong Delta.

In February 1972, the 147th and 258th Brigades were on the DMZ in Quang Tri Province, along with the green 3rd ARVN Division. The brigades were defending west and south of Quang Tri City. The 147th's 4th Battalion was guarding the far west approaches, the 8th Battalion east of the 4th along the Thach Han River, and the 1st Battalion further east. The 258th was in reserve south of Quang Tri City and the 359th was in strategic reserve in the Saigon area.

On 30 March 1972, the NVA launched a well coordinated three divisional attack across the DMZ supported by artillery and over 400 tanks. The ARVN 3rd Division, not expecting an attack across the DMZ, was routed. Coinciding with the DMZ attack, the NVA attacked from the west against the 8th Marine Battalion. Several platoon and squad sized positions outside the perimeter were overrun by human wave assaults. Also, several fire support bases of the 4th Battalion were overrun after intense artillery, rocket and mortar fire. Nui Ba Ho, Sarge and Holcomb were lost. Only 69 of more than 300 Marines at NBH made it back to friendly lines. During the early NVA attack, weather prevented close VNAF/USAF air support.

The 258th Brigade was ordered to displace to Dong Ha on the evening of 30 March and on the first moved to the combat base at Ai Tu. After the initial NVA attacks, the RVNAF defensive line was along the Cam Lo-Cau Viet Rivers and in the west the Cam Lo-Mai Loc vicinity. Headquarters, 147th Brigade was at Mai Loc. Its 4th Battalion was badly battered, but the 7th and 8th Battalions were in good shape despite NVA artillery attacks. On Easter Sunday, 2 April, the 3rd Battalion around Dong Ha reported a column of enemy tanks moving down Route 1. If the tanks crossed the Dong Ha Bridge, the RVNAF in Quang Tri Province were lost. The 3rd Battalion moved into defensive positions around the bridge and a LAW (Light Anti-tank Weapon) team fired two rockets at the lead tank. The first missed, but the second scored, only inflicting minor damage. The tank commander was so surprised that he backed up thus ending the enemy's tank attack to conquer Quang Tri and advance

toward Hue. Later two American Advisors, one Army, the other Marine, blew the Dong Ha Bridge. The 3rd Battalion and the ARVN 20th Tank Battalion continued to engage the tanks along Route 1 destroying two. The NVA had over 100 tanks and 5 regiments of infantry ready to cross the river.

To the west, the RVNAF was receiving intensive enemy artillery fire and in the afternoon, the 2,000-man 56th Infantry at Camp Carroll surrendered without contest. By the end of Easter Sunday, the 3rd ARVN Division was down to two effective infantry battalions. The 57th Infantry, along with civilians spent most of the day fleeing down Route 1 under severe NVA artillery fire.

After the surrender of Camp Carroll, the Marine position at Mai Loc was untenable. Under cover of darkness the 147th Brigade with its 4th, 7th and 8th Infantry battalions and the 2nd Artillery Battalion pulled out and by the following afternoon reached Route 1. At this time, the 258th Brigade was at Ai Tu with the 1st and 6th Battalions defending to the west.

On 3 April, the 369th Brigade landed at Phu Bai and moved to the northern boundary of Thua Thien Province, the My Chanh River. They would later save the Marines and ARVN in Quang Tri Province.

The 3rd Battalion was ordered back to Ai Tu to relieve the 6th on 8 April. The 6th moved six miles southwest and occupied FB Pedro. On the night of the 8th, the 6th Battalion received intensive NVA artillery fire, which pretty much reduced the FB to rubble. At dawn, the NVA launched a tank attack supported by infantry. Marine artillery fire eliminated the infantry, however, the NVA tanks continued to roll on towards Ai Tu. Pedro defenders destroyed some tanks with LAWS; others hit mines and were disabled. Meanwhile, a Marine counterattack force was organized at Ai Tu. It consisted of the 1st Battalion and elements of the ARVN 20th Tank Battalion. This force advanced on line and took the NVA T-54 tanks under fire, destroying several, while other NVA were destroyed by anti-tank mines. The counterattack, supported by VNAF, was a complete success. A total of 23 NVA tanks were destroyed and many more suffered damage.

Again, on the 18th, the NVA attacked all along the western line with infantry and tanks supported by artillery. The 3rd and 6th Battalions of the 258th joined in repulsing the attack. On 22 April the 147th Brigade, which had been refitted at Hue, relieved the 258th. The 147th consisted of the 1st, 4th and 8th Infantry battalions and the 1st Artillery Battalion, all fresh and ready to get at the NVA which continued their in-depth artillery fire, and on the 27th launched a major drive toward Quang Tri City. Once again, refugees took to Route 1, creating confusion. In the west, the 1st and 8th Battalions held but because adjacent ARVN units didn't, were forced to fall back. The 7th Battalion of the 369th was sent to QT City but was ambushed and only two companies reached Ai Tu. The NVA attacks were generally successful and only the 147th at Ai Tu was holding their ground but under attack from three sides.

By 30 April, enemy artillery fire was so intense on the 147th that it was decided to abandon Ai Tu and pull back to Quang Tri City. Unfortunately ARVN engineers had blown all the bridges into the city, thus the artillery was forced to destroy all guns and vehicles and the 147th had to wade across the Thach Han. Some drowned, but the brigade made a successful crossing and became the only defenders of the city as ARVN forces were in full retreat. On 1 May under USAF cover, the 147th evacuated the city. The 3rd Division Headquarters accompanied them. By nightfall, they reached Hai Lang and radio communication was made with the 369th. It was decided to wait until dawn to make a dash for the My Chanh River and the 369th. Enemy armor was seen the next morning, but the column began to move. Route 1 was filled with thousands of South Vietnamese trying to make the My Chanh Bridge. It was touch and go but on 2 June, the 147th crossed the My Chanh.

The 369th consisted of the 2nd, 5th and 9th Battalions. They had fought a series of battles in southern Quang Tri Province to keep Route 1 open. They were in constant contact with the NVA and on 2 May the 9th Battalion, deployed along the O'Khe River, repelled a superior NVA force, thus allowing the fleeing South Vietnamese to cross the My Chanh to safety.

The NVA launched several major attacks against the My Chanh line in May. All were repulsed with heavy NVA losses. Meanwhile, the RVNAF were preparing for the recapture of Quang Tri Province. The Marines launched two attacks behind enemy lines. The first was just north of the My Chanh, an airmobile assault using U.S. Navy choppers. The second assault was at Wunder Beach. These assaults disrupted NVA supply lines, terrorized rear echelon units and attacked the NVA front lines from the rear.

On 28 June, the main RVNAF attack to retake Quang Tri Province was made by the Airborne Division on the left and the Marine Division on the right. The NVA was routed and fell back to Quang Tri City. The Marines staged another behind the lines assault on 11 July, this time north of Quang Tri City. A three-day battle followed which resulted in the RVNAF occupying three sides of the Citadel. On 9 September, the 147th and 258th launched attacks and the 6th Battalion was the first unit to enter the Citadel. It was closely followed by the 3rd. At noon on the 16th, the RVN flag was raised over the Citadel. In the campaign from the My Chanh to the recapture of the Citadel, the Marines suffered about 20 percent casualties in killed and wounded.

Retaking the Citadel ended the RVNAF offensive. Consequently, the NVA controlled all territory north of the Thach Han River and all of western Quang Tri Province. For the remainder of 1972, all of 1973 and to June 1974 the Marine Division remained in Quang Tri Province,

defending along the Thach Han to the sea and along the western approaches to Route 1. This area remained quiet and the morale of the Marines was the best in the RVNAF. No fighting and brigades were rotated back and forth between Saigon and Quang Tri.

By June 1974, the Division was extended south to cover 10 km of Thua Thien. While all was quiet in Quang Tri, the NVA were on the attack elsewhere in MR-I and there were not enough RVNAF troops to defend the country. Severe cutbacks in military aid from the U.S. also limited TAC air and artillery support. In addition, many vehicles were deadlined for lack of spare parts. Nonetheless, the Marines continued to display high morale and a keen sense of duty.

In January 1975, the 147th assumed responsibility for the area west of Hue. The Division pulled two battalions out of forward positions northwest of Hue to form a heavier reserve for the I Corps Commander and the JGS. Later in January, Marine positions in Quang Tri were occupied by RF battalions. The three Marine battalions shifted south to Thua Thien Province.

The NVA attacked the Song Bo corridor with infantry and tanks on 10 March. The 147th Brigade, containing the 3rd, 4th, 5th and 7th Battalions, fought well and repulsed enemy attacks for two days. Although the Marines inflicted heavy casualties on the NVA, the ARVN and Territorials crumpled under the attacks. As a result the Marines pulled back to defend Danang, leaving only the 369th above the Hai Van Pass. The Division CP was set up on Marble Mountain on 18 March. As matters deteriorated in MR-I the 147th and 258th withdrew to Danang and sailed for Vung Tau. They remained a disciplined and cohesive unit throughout the debacle in MR-I. On 2 April, the survivors reached Vung Tau. From a strength of 12,000 prior to the NVA final offensive, about 4,000 Marines got off the boats at Vung Tau.

The Marine Training Center was located at Di An, about halfway between Saigon and Bien Hoa. Brigades rotated here from Quang Tri for rest and retraining. The last Division Commander was BG Bui The Lan.

"We have sometimes been weak and sometimes powerful, but at no time have we suffered from a lack of heroes."

—*Vietnamese emperor Le Loi, 1428*

Landing a Vietnamese Marine Battalion near Hue-1967. Notice the mixture of uniforms and the support required.

On his visit to the Republic of Vietnam, General Robert E. Cushman, Jr., Commandant of the Marine Corps, is briefed on RVN Marine Corps operations at the old imperial capital of Hue, now headquarters of the 1st Division. Shown arriving at the briefing are (left to right) General Cushman, Colonel J.W. Dorsey III, senior Marine (USMC) advisor in Military Region One, RVN, Brigadier General Bui The Laan, Commandant, RVN Marine Corps, Lieutenant Colonel Dwayne Gray, Officer in Charge, Sub-Unit #1, ANGLICO, RVN, and Brigadier General E.J. Miller, Commanding General, 9th Marine Amphibious Brigade; June 1972.

AWARDS, INSIGNIA, FLAGS AND UNIFORMS

A badge, unit insignia, flags, streamers and uniforms are a source of pride for military personnel of all nations—it sets them apart. The combatant relates his assignments, experiences, and hardships to these items of military heredity; he will—and has—given his life to defend the unit colors or the nation's flag. Prisoners of war (POWs) have risked their lives while in captivity displaying the flag. Though most are artistic symbols of the deeds and honors established by the unit, their purpose is to identify an individual with his regiment, to foster military tradition and *esprit dé corps.*

The republic of Vietnam created their awards system after the French with added patriotic and valor influence as the war expanded, as so with their military flags and guidons, which were symbolic of the type of unit. Vietnam's flag of imperial gold with three red horizontal stripes representing the traditional regions of the country was the backbone of its people and the ARVN armed forces. The Marines raising the "flag" at Quang Tri, is tangible evidence of honor, country (fatherland), and duty. To this day, the Vietnamese veterans and their families respect and honor the South Vietnamese flag—it is their link to their ancestral past, to their homeland.

American officers and enlisted men were authorized some Vietnamese awards, and American units that distinguished themselves were presented Vietnamese Unit Awards. Advisors serving with ARVN units at the time of the recognition were authorized to receive and wear the Vietnamese unit awards—an acknowledgement of those who lived, fought, and sometimes died with their counterparts.

Vietnamese Marine Veterans at ceremonies in California.

Enlarged Division Pool

Brigade S.S.I.

Division S.S.I.

Division Pocket Insignia

A Brigade (LU DOAN Brigade)

B Brigade (BAC BINH VUONG – King Nguyen Hue conquered the North in 1789)

Officer's Cap Badge

Medical Battalion

Signal Battalion
(TRUYEN SONG - Tidal Waves)

Transportation Battalion
(HUU-HIEN, Efficiency and
CHIEN-THANG, Victory)

1st Artillery Battalion
(Lighting Fire)

2nd Artillery Battalion
(Sacred Arrow)

3rd Artillery Battalion
(Sacred Bow)

3rd Battalion
(SOI BIEN - Sea Wolf)

1st Battalion
(QUAI-DIEU, Monster Bird)

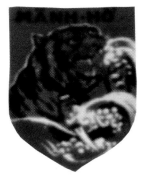

9th Battalion
(MANH-HO, Strong Tiger)

2nd Battalion
(TRAU DIEN, Crazy Buffalo)

Division S.S.I.

8th Battalion
(Ó-BIEN, Sea Hawk)

4th Battalion
(KINH-NGU, Killer Fish)

5th Battalion
(HAC LONG, Black Dragon)

6th Battalion
(THAN-UNG, Sacred Bird
and CAM-TU, Suicide)

7th Battalion
(HUM XAM, Killer Tiger)

Pocket Insignia - DANH DU TO QUOC and
THUY QUAN LUC CHIEN (Marine Infantry)

Pocket Insignia - hand embroidered

Signal Battalion

Signal Battalion (Variation)

USMC Advisors to RVN Marine Corps (RUNG SAT Special
Zone) printed patch, not authorized, but designed and worn
by Marine Advisors in the RUNG SAT area of operations.

Lapel brass for Marine Officer – bright brass

Lapel brass for Marine NCO – blackened, also in silver for NCOs

Metal Officer beret badge

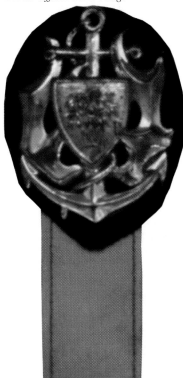

Heavy Wire Dress Officer's peaked cap badge – Rare

Beret Badge – cloth embroidery on red background

Beret Badge – wire embroidery on green background, note: eagle looks to his right

Beret Badge – cloth embroidery on green background

Officer peaked cap metal badge

NCO peaked cap metal badge (silver)

Officer's Beret Badge (gold)

NCO Beret Badge (silver in large and small size). Note: these are old versions of the cap and beret badges; design is an anchor with line, waves, and shield with bamboo trees.

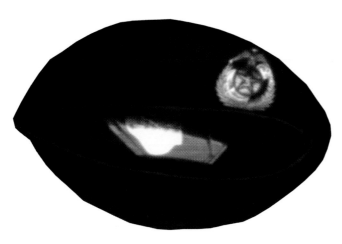

Green (made by Hieu SU-TU, Saigon) with Officers' Beret Badge

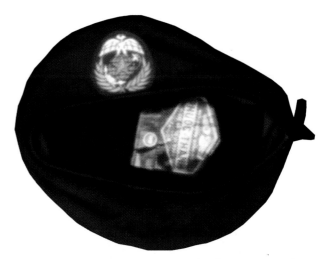

*Green (made by PHUOC-THANH) with Officers' Beret Badge
(red background)*

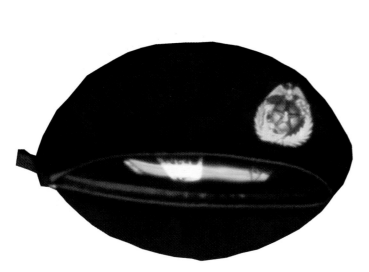

*Green (made by CHAN-HUNG) with Enlisted Beret Badge
(red background)*

Medium Green (made by CHAN-HUNG) with sewn Officer's patch

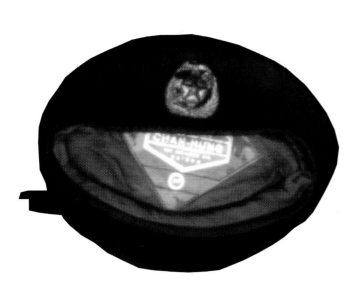

Dark Green (made by CHAN-HUNG) with enlisted metal badge

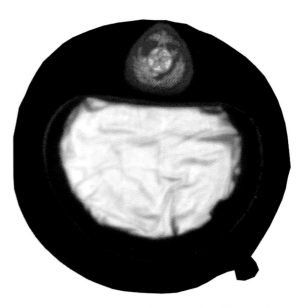

Dark Green (French made type) with Bullion Patch.

Black "BATA" boots

Green boots

Tiger Stripe (not "official" Marine pattern - sea wave) shirt with pocket patch, 1st BN shoulder patch, Marine Division shoulder patch, and basic para wings; utility cap (cover) in "official" Marine pattern camo, with metal 2nd LT rank badge on front.

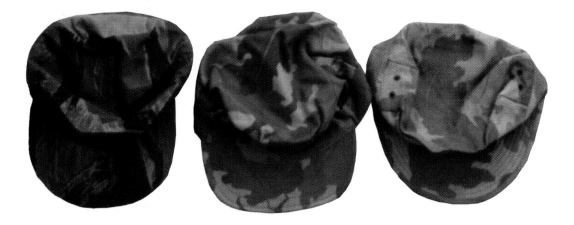

Left to right: RVNMC Naval Covers: ARVN tiger stripe material; USMC Camo Cover (made "in-country" from US camo material); Camo helmet covers (US Army style).

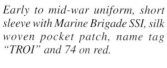

Early to mid-war uniform, short sleeve with Marine Brigade SSI, silk woven pocket patch, name tag "TROI" and 74 on red.

Mid-war, "Sea Wave" light weight uniform with cover.

Late-war, light weight uniform with "boonie hat" – 5th BN SSI, Division SSI, and pocket patch.

Commander's Flag

Commander's Guidon

Division/Brigade Guidon

Officer's School Guidon

NCO School Guidon

Alpha (A) Brigade Guidon

1st BN Guidon (Monster Bird)

2nd Battalion Guidon (Crazy Buffalos)

3rd Battalion Guidon (Sea Wolves)

4th Battalion Guidon (Killer Fish)

6th Battalion Guidon (Suicidal Sacred Falcon)

8th Battalion Guidon (Sea Hawk)

1st ARTY Battalion Guidon (Lighting Fire)

2nd ARTY Battalion Guidon (Sacred Arrow)

Vietnamese Military Awards

The ribbons and their devices are in the correct order that they are worn on the military uniform.

National Order Of Vietnam	Bao-Quoc Huan-Chuong
Military Merit Medal	Quan-Cong Boi-Tinh
Army Distinguished Service Order	Luc-Quan Huan-Chuong
Air Force Distinguished Service Order	Khong-Luc Huan-Chuong
Navy Distinguished Service Order	Hai-Quan Huan-Chuong
Army Meritorious Service Medal	Luc-Quan Vinh-Cong Boi-Tinh
Air Force Meritorious Service Medal	Khong-Quan Vinh-Cong Boi-Tinh
Navy Meritorious Service Medal	Hai-Quan Vinh-Cong Boi-Tinh
Special Service Medal	Biet-Cong Boi-Tinh
Gallantry Cross	Anh-Dung Boi-Tinh
Air Gallantry Cross	Phi-Dung Boi-Tinh
Navy Gallantry Cross	Hai-Dung Boi-Tinh
Hazardous Service Medal	Uu- Dung Boi-Tinh
Life Saving Medal	Nhan- Dung Boi-Tinh
Loyalty Medal	Trung-Chanh Boi-Tinh
Wound Medal	Chien-Thuong Boi-Tinh
Armed Forces Honor Medal	Danh-Du Boi-Tinh
Leadership Medal	Chi-Dao Boi-Tinh
Staff Service Medal	Tham-Muu Boi-Tinh
Technical Service Medal	Ky-Thuat Boi-Tinh
Training Service Medal	Huan-Vu Boi-Tinh
Civil Actions Medal	Dan-Vu Boi-Tinh
Good Conduct Medal	Quan-Phong Boi-Tinh
Campaign Medal	Chien-Dich Boi-Tinh
Military Service Medal	Quan-Vu Boi-Tinh
Air Service Medal	Khong-Vu Boi-Tinh
Navy Service Medal	Hai-Vu Boi-Tinh

Vietnamese Civilian Awards

The ribbons and their devices are in the correct order that they are worn by civilians.

National Order Of Vietnam	Bao-Quoc Huan-Chuong
Kim Khanh Medal	Kim-Khanh
Chuong My Medal	Chuong-My Boi-Tinh
Administrative Service Medal	Hanh-Chanh Boi-Tinh
Dedicated Service Medal	Nghia-Vu Boi-Tinh
Justice Medal	Tu-Phap Boi-Tinh
Cultural and Educational Service Medal	Boi-Tinh Van-Hoa Giao Duc
Public Health Service Medal	Y-Te Boi-Tinh
Social Service Medal	Xa-Hoi Boi-Tinh
Economic Service Medal	Kinh-Te Boi-Tinh
Finance Service Medal	Boi-Tinh Tai-Chanh
Psychological Warfare Medal	Boi-Tinh Tam Ly-Chien
Agricultural Service Medal	Nong-Nghiep Boi-Tinh
Public Works, Communication and Transportation Service Medal	Boi-Tinh Cong-Chanh va Giao Thong Van-Tai
Labor Medal	Lao-Dong Boi-Tinh
Rural Revolutionary Development Medal	Xay-Dung Nong-Thon Boi-Tinh
Ethnic Development Service Medal	Boi-Tinh Phat-Trien Sac-Toc
Veterans Medal	Cuu-Chien Binh Boi-Tinh
Police Merit Medal	Canh-Sat Chien-Du Boi-Tinh
Police Honor Medal	Canh-Sat Danh-Du Boi-Tinh
People's Self-Defense Medal	Boi-Tinh Nhan-Dan Tu Ve
Youth And Sports Service Medal	Boi-Tinh Thanh-Nien The Thao
Hamlet Common Defense Medal	Boi-Tinh Toan-Dan Bao-Ve Non-Song

MARINES IN UNIFORM

Colonel L.V. Corbett, presenting the "Purple Heart" to Captain John J. Sheehan, who was wounded while serving as an Advisor to the 2nd Battalion, VNMC. Sheehan went on to achieve the rank of a 4 star General.

ROKMC Sergeant Major Kim Duk Saeng, marches in a ceremonial parade with the United Nations' Honor Guard in Seoul, Korea in 1978; he wears the ROKMC white dress uniform. Kim served with the Korean Marines in Vietnam and was liaison to a Vietnamese Marine unit. The Republic of Korea Marine Corps was a part of the allied forces that fought in South Vietnam.

Center: Colonel James T. Breckinridge, flanked by Colonel Corbett on the right and VNMC Chief of Staff (then), Colonel Bui The Lan on the left. Breckinridge had just been promoted to Colonel and had been presented with "shoulder boards" by Col. Lan. Colonel Breckinridge had been assigned to Vietnam in 1955, with a noncommissioned officer, Technical Sergeant Jackson E. Tracy. The two Advisors were assigned to TRIM (a combined Franco-American training command, designated the Training Relations Instruction Mission). Breckinridge would replace the French Army Captain, Jean Louis Delayen, as the Advisor to the Vietnamese 1st Marine Landing Battalion (or 1st Landing Battalion).

General Jean Louis DeLayen, a French Marine, was the commander of the 1st Marine Landing Battalion when it was formed at Nha Trang in 1954. He later became the only French Advisor – and the last – to the Vietnamese Marines. General DeLayen served three tours in Indochina; he also fought in WWII, Algeria, and Chad, receiving three combat wounds. He was awarded the French Grand Cross de La Legion d'Honor.

Colonel Lance V. Corbett, Advisor to the Vietnamese Marine Corps, in khaki dress uniform with service cap.

Lieutenant Luong Nguyen, San Jose, California – 1999. Luong graduated from the Vietnamese National Military Academy in 1972, and was assigned to the 3rd Battalion, VNMC. The battalion was defending the Dong Ha-Cam Lo intersection near the Dong Ha Bridge that was destroyed by Captain Ripley. He remembers the North Vietnamese trying to infiltrate their positions by intermingling with the civilians fleeing the area... too, he vividly recalls an occasion when the Marines and the North Vietnamese each, attempted to claim a dead cow that was strategically positioned between the opposing forces – "to the victor goes the spoils."

Office of LtGen Anthony Lukeman, who wrote the final report on the Vietnamese Marine Corps; left Vietnam in the spring of 1975.

Brothers-in-Arms: Vietnamese Marines pose for a photograph. Note the red "name tags" identifying them as members of the 4th VNMC Battalion.

Captain Robinson in the "sea wave" camouflage uniform. He is wearing both American and Vietnamese rank insignia.

The US Silver Star award is presented to Cpl Phuoc-VNMC, for his conspicuous gallantry in action with the 2nd Battalion, by Lieutenant General Lewis W. Walt – then-Major General – Commander, U.S. III Marine Amphibious Force and the I Corps senior advisor. The American military awarded both individual and unit awards to the Vietnamese; they presented theirs to the Americans and other allied units.

Captain Nguyen Tien Tan (center) attended the Basic Course in the United Sates, 1968; received an honorary life membership from the Fredericksburg Chamber of Commerce. As a First Lieutenant, Tan was awarded the US Silver Star for "gallantry in action" on 21 September 1968.

VIỆT-NAM CỘNG HÒA
QUÂN LỰC VIỆT-NAM CỘNG HÒA

LỮ ĐOÀN THỦY QUÂN LỤC CHIẾN
Tiểu Đoàn 2
❦

– *Tham chiếu thông tư số 71/QP ngày 20-1-1953*
– *Tham chiếu nghị định số 282/QP/NĐ ngày 19-4-1966.*
   Cho phép TĐ2/TQLC được mang giây BIỂU CHƯƠNG màu
   QUÂN CÔNG BỘI TINH.

CHỨNG NHẬN Số 041

Tiểu Đoàn Trưởng Tiểu Đoàn 2/TQLC
   Chứng nhận : Thg/Sĩ 1 NGÔ-VĂN-XUYÊN   Số quân : 44A/102.006
đã góp công trong chiến thắng mà TIỂU ĐOÀN 2/TQLC. 4 lần được tuyên dương công
trạng trước QUÂN ĐỘI và được mang giây Biểu Chương màu QUÂN CÔNG BỘI TINH.

   Chứng nhận này cho phép đương sự được mang giây Biểu Chương cá nhân
theo các điều khoản trong thông tư tham chiếu.

            K.B.C 3.335, ngày 01 tháng 04 năm 1967

                   Thiếu-Tá NGÔ-VĂN-ĐỊNH
                   Tiểu-Đoàn-Trưởng
                   Tiểu Đoàn 2 Thủy Quân Lục-Chiến

REPUBLIC OF VIETNAM
ARMED FORCES OF THE REPUBLIC OF VIETNAM

BRIGADE OF MARINES
2ND BATTALION

   -As per notice No.71/National Defense,of 20 January 1953
   -As per Decree No.282/National Defense Decision of 19 April 1966
   Grants permission to the 2nd Battalion of Marines to
   wear the fourregere in the colors of THE MILITARY MERIT MEDAL.

        CERTIFICATE NUMBER   041

        The commander of the 2nd Battalion of Marines
certifies that:Adjutant 1st Class NGÔ-VAN-XUYÊN Military I.D.No.:44A/102,006
had contributed to the victory which gave the 2nd Battalion of Marines the
occasion to be mentioned in despatches before the Army 4 times which
accorded them permission to wear the fourregere in the colors of THE
MILITARY MERIT MEDAL.

        This certificate permits the bearer to wear, as his personal
decoration,the fourregere conforming to the notice referenced above.

                   APO 3.335,the 1st of April 1967
                   Major NGÔ-VĂN-ĐỊNH
                   Commanding the
                   2nd Marine Battalion

MEDAL OF HONOR AND NAVY CROSS CITATIONS

The President of the United States in the name of The Congress takes pride in presenting the Medal of Honor posthumously to:

COLONEL DONALD G. COOK
UNITED STATES MARINE CORPS

for service as set forth in the following

CITATION

For conspicuous gallantry and intrepidity at the risk of his life above and beyond the call of duty while interned as a Prisoner of War by the Viet Cong in the Republic of Vietnam during the period 31 December 1964 to 8 December 1967. Despite the fact that by doing so he knew he would bring about harsher treatment for himself, Colonel (then Captain) Cook established himself as a senior prisoner, even though in actuality he was not. Repeatedly assuming more than his share of the manual labor in order that the other Prisoners Of War could improve the state of their health, Colonel Cook willingly as unselfishly put the interests of his comrades before that of his own well–being and, eventually, his life. Giving more needy men his medicine and drug allowance while constantly nursing them, he risked infection from contagious diseases while in a rapidly deteriorating state of health. This unselfish and exemplary conduct, coupled with his refusal to stray even the slightest from the Code Of Conduct, earned him the deepest respect from not only his fellow prisoners, but his captors as well. Rather than negotiate for his own release or better treatment, he steadfastly frustrated attempts by the Viet Cong to break his indomitable spirit, and passed this same resolve on to the men with whose well–being he so closely associated himself. Knowing his refusals would prevent has release prior to the end of the war, and also knowing his chances for prolonged survival would be small in the event of continued refusal, he chose nevertheless to adhere to a Code Of Conduct far above that which could be expected. His personal valor and exceptional spirit of loyalty in the face of almost certain death reflected the highest credit upon Colonel Cook, the Marine Corps, and the United States Naval Service.

Colonel Donald C. Cook. Cook was the first Marine captured during the Vietnam War. His experiences and efforts as a POW gained him the Medal of Honor even though he never returned. He was a captain at the time of his capture, serving with the 4th Vietnamese Marine Battalion at the battle of Binh Gia – he was OJT from Okinawa. Sergeant Harold G. Bennett, an Army Ranger Advisor, was a prisoner with Cook; Bennett was executed by the Viet Cong.

The President of the United States takes pride in presenting the Navy Cross to:

CAPTAIN LAWRENCE H. LIVINGSTON
UNITED STATES MARINE CORPS

For service as set forth in the following

CITATION

For extraordinary heroism on 11 July 1972 while serving as Senior Advisor to the 1st Vietnamese Marine Corps Infantry Battalion during a heliborne assault into enemy-held territory northeast of Quang Tri City, Republic of Vietnam. When the battalion encountered unexpectedly heavy enemy fire while disembarking into the landing zone, and sustained numerous casualties, Captain Livingston moved throughout the hasty positions taken by the scattered and hesitant element and formed the Marines into an assault force. Despite the continuing heavy concentration of hostile fire, he began the assault on the initial objective—a treeline approximately 50 yards distant. Although blown from his feet by explosions, and periodically delayed to reform and redirect his casualty-riddled force, he forged ahead, leading the Vietnamese Marines into the enemy-infested trench lines of the objective and a subsequent hands-to-hand battle. Upon seizure of the initial portion of the trenchline, Captain Livingston shed his combat equipment, emerged from the trenchline, and exposed himself to a hail of enemy fire to reach and carry his wounded naval gunfire spotter to a position of relative safety. Captain Livingston's repeated acts of heroism in the face of heavy fire reflected great credit upon him and the Marine Corps and were in keeping with the highest traditions of the United States Naval Service.

The President of the United States takes pleasure in presenting the Navy Cross to:

CAPTAIN RAY L. SMITH
UNITED STATES MARINE CORPS

For service as set forth in the following

CITATION

For extraordinary heroism during the period 30 March to 1 April 1972 while serving as advisor to a Vietnamese command group, numbering approximately 250 Vietnamese Marines located on a small hilltop outpost in the Republic of Vietnam. With the command group repulsing several savage enemy assaults, and subjected to a continuing hail of fire from an attacking force estimated to be of two-battalion strength, Captain Smith repeatedly exposed himself to the heavy fire while directing friendly air support. When adverse weather conditions precluded further close air support, he attempted to lead the group, now reduced to only 28 Vietnamese Marines, to the safety of friendly lines. An enemy soldier opened fire upon the Marines at the precise moment that they had balked when encountering an outer defense ring of barbed wire. Captain Smith returned accurate fire, disposing of the attacker, and then threw himself backwards on top of the booby-trap-infested wire barrier. Swiftly, the remaining Marines moved over the crushed wire, stepping on Captain Smith's prostate body, until all had passed safely through the barrier. Although suffering severe cuts and bruises, Captain Smith succeeded in leading the Marines to the safety of friendly lines. His great personal valor and unrelenting devotion to duty reflected the highest credit upon himself, the Marine Corps, and the United States Naval Service.

The President of the United States takes pleasure in presenting the Navy Cross to:

CAPTAIN JOHN W. RIPLEY
UNITED STATES MARINE CORPS

for service as set forth in the following

CITATION

For extraordinary heroism on 2 April 1972 while serving as a Senior Marine Advisor to the 3rd Vietnamese Marine Corps Infantry Battalion in the Republic of Vietnam. Upon receipt of a report that a rapidly moving, mechanized, North Vietnamese Army force, estimated at a reinforced divisional strength, was attacking south along Route 1, the 3d Vietnamese Marine Infantry Battalion was positioned to defend a key village and the surrounding area. It became imperative that a vital river bridge be destroyed if the overall security of the northern provinces of Military Region 1 was to be maintained. Advancing to the bridge to personally supervise this most dangerous but vitally important assignment, Captain Ripley located a large amount of explosives which had been prepositioned their earlier, access to which was blocked by a chain-link fence. In order to reposition the approximately 500 pounds of explosives, Captain Ripley was obliged to reach up and hand-walk along the beams while his body dangled beneath the bridge. On five separate occasions, in the face of constant enemy fire, he moved to points along the bridge and with the aid of another advisor, who pushed the explosives to him, securely emplaced them. He detonated the charges and destroyed the bridge, thereby stopping the enemy assault. By his heroic actions and extraordinary courage, Captain Ripley undoubtedly was instrumental in saving an untold number of lives. His inspiring efforts reflected great credit upon himself, the Marine Corps, and the United States Naval Service.

Assistant Commandant VNMC, Bui The Lan, presents a Vietnamese award to Marine Advisor, Captain Bernis B. Conatser.

Colonel Tri, VNMC G–3, after presenting a Vietnamese award to Marine Advisor, Major Ernest G. Rivers.

In a hidden base camp, Viet Cong pose for a photograph; their equipment includes AK47 weapons and US radios.

THE ENEMY WE FACE

USARV Information Office (1969)

"They came to my house and told my mother that I had been chosen to be one of them. They wanted me to become a *Chien Si* (soldier). My mother pleaded that I was too young. The North Vietnamese soldiers said, 'He is old enough—the draft age is 15 to 40.'"

This is how fifteen-year-old Nguyen Van Qui became one of the enemy you faced. His story is typical. He was then taken to a training camp near Com Ninh, in the Southern Panhandle of North Vietnam. There, he and other recruits were given their khaki uniforms and taught to aim and fire a weapon. The complete training cycle for duty as a regular Chien Si in the North Vietnamese Army (NVA) lasted six days.

After his training, Qui and 1,200 others were sent on a four-week journey down the Ho Chi Minh Trail. They moved in small groups to escape B-52 raids. About 700 of them were armed.

"Many died on the trail," Qui recalled. "Some died of malaria and others died of not enough food. It was very hard. Everybody was sick, but they kept pushing us."

The NVA now comprises perhaps over half of the total enemy forces in the Republic of Vietnam, with their percentage growing smaller as one travels toward the Mekong Delta. They depend upon infiltrated units for reinforcements and resupply, and fewer paid anything more than a bag of salt for their efforts. Each unit has a political officer who tries to maintain morale with a steady flow of North Vietnamese ideology.

Still they often pose a more formidable threat on the battlefield than do the Viet Cong, who fill the remaining ranks of the enemy. This elusive, so-called Liberation Army consists of two basic elements—the paramilitary and the full military.

The paramilitary Viet Cong is generally a local civilian who is a part-time soldier, whose military duties do not take him far from home. In addition, he is not highly indoctrinated politically. The Liberation Front calls this force the Guerrilla Popular Army (GPA); at the hamlet level the GPA unit is either a cell, a half squad or squad—three, six or twelve men. The GPA unit at the village level, consisting of several hamlets, is the platoon, made up of three or four squads—36 or 48 men.

There are two basic classes of GPA members. The first is the Viet Cong in the village, frequently an older man, who is generally used as a village defender. He has little training and is armed with scanty or primitive weapons. The second is the Viet Cong combat soldier, who is younger and better trained and armed. He is frequently called upon to aid mobile columns or fill military units in the vicinity of his village or hamlet. The VC combat units also serve as manpower pools for the Viet Cong's full military units.

The full military element also is divided into two types—the Regional Forces and the Main Force. They're not organized or operated like an orthodox army. Their units are self-contained, not uniformed and rely primarily on guerrilla-type tactics. They depend on local populations for much of their logistical support.

The Regional Forces, also called Territorials are units established by Front district committees, which provide their leadership and direct their activities. A Regional Force operates mostly in one area.

The elite units of the Viet Cong are the battalions of the Main Force. They have acquired the name of "hard hats" because of the metal or fiberboard helmets that distinguish them from the Regional Forces and paramilitary VC. These battalions are directed by the Front committees at the provincial level and range farther afield in their combat operations.

During the early days of the conflict, the Communists fought with older weapons used in previous wars by the French, Japanese and Americans. But today, largely as a result of aid from Red China and the Soviet Union, North Vietnamese Army troops and many main-force Viet Cong units are equipped with late model weapons comparable to those used by U.S. forces.

The most common of these are the SKS carbine, the Soviet AK-47 assault rifle, or—more often—a Chinese copy of either. These weapons use identical 7.62 mm rounds, similar to the round fired by the U.S. M-14 rifle, but shorter. Both have a maximum effective range of 400 m. The assault rifle most often captured is the Chicom (short for "Chinese Communist") Type 56, although soldiers in the field usually refer to it as the AK-47, since it is a virtual copy of that weapon. It can be fired on automatic at a rate of 150 rounds a minute, or on semi-automatic.

The SKS Carbine—or the Chicom 7.62 copy—is a semi-automatic weapon. It weighs nearly nine pounds when loaded with a ten–round magazine.

Until three years ago, the only machine guns available to the VC were obsolete French, Chinese and German models. Today, however, each NVA and Main Force VC battalion is allocated 36 light machine guns, usually the 7.62 mm Type 56 RPD or the older and heavier Type 58 RD46. Both can accurately fire 150 rounds a minute up to ranges of 800 meters. These automatic weapons were first supplied to the North Vietnamese in 1965.

A weapon which the enemy has been using with growing frequency, especially in stand off attacks on U.S. and Republic of Vietnam military bases, is the mortar. Standard mortars in Charlie's arsenal are the 82 mm—backbone of his high-angle fire support—and the 60 mm, normally used in small-scale guerrilla actions.

Ready to fire, the 60mm mortar weighs 45 lbs and its 3.2 lb. projectile travels up to 1,500 meters. The 82 mm in firing position weighs 123 lbs and hurls a 6.72-pound projectile at targets up to 3,040 meters away.

The 82 mm round was designed 1 mm larger than the U.S. 81 mm round so the Communists can employ captured U.S. mortar rounds in their tubes.

During early 1968, a 120 mm mortar, capable of hurling a 33.9-lb warhead 5,700 meters, was added to the Communist arsenal. With a total weight of 606 lbs, it is more difficult to transport and is not widely used.

The enemy also has stepped up his use of rockets within the past year. Charlie employs rockets in stand off attacks of military installations and as general support artillery.

The simple but effective Soviet-made 122 mm rocket launcher, first used in Vietnam in May 1967, can hurl with area target accuracy a projectile weighing more than 100 pounds up to ranges of 11,000 meters.

The 140 mm rocket, with a carrying weight of 88 pounds and a projectile weight of 70 pounds has a range of 9,500 meters. This rocket was first employed in an attack on Danang, February 1968. Its use thus far has been largely restricted to the northern I Corps Tactical Zone, primarily because of logistical limitations.

The latest type of rocket introduced by the enemy is the Chinese-made 107 mm, which weighs less than half as much as either of the others and has an estimated effective range of 9,000 meters.

In 1965, the enemy added to his grenade capability with the introduction of the Soviet-made RPG-2 anti-tank grenade launcher. Two years later the RPG-7 appeared.

The RPG-2 has a maximum effective range of 150 meters and can penetrate 6-7 in. of armor. The RPG-7, with an improved side, is affective up to 500 meters and can penetrate steel 12-14 inches thick.

Probably the most striking recent addition to the enemy arsenal is the Soviet PT-76—an amphibious tank equipped with a 76 mm gun capable of firing 25 rounds a minute at ranges up to 13,300 meters. Highly maneuverable with its hydro-jet propulsion system, it can cross waterways at 6 miles an hour and has a cruising range of 155 miles.

AMBUSH AT SONG O LAU

Marine Tom Campbell

"Trau Dien" is Vietnamese "Crazy Water Buffalo," and the happy warriors of the 2nd Battalion, Vietnamese Marine Brigade took pride in that name and the buffalo head shoulder patch they sported on their tiger-striped uniforms. The battalion, it was said, fought like demented or crazed buffaloes. The Marines were also proud of their twelve-year combat record and the fact that they were one of the first Vietnamese units to be recommended for the U.S. Presidential Unit Citation—a recommendation won after an earlier all-night battle in which the battalion had fought off six enemy assaults before recoiling from a seventh attack with a slashing counterattack that had forced a Viet Cong retreat.

They were proud, too, of their little, mustachioed battalion commander, whose light heart and fondness for guitar playing and singing had given them a battle song which was theirs alone, unique among the other battalions of the VNMB. They knew that Trung Ta Minh's blithe spirit concealed a combat toughness and professional skill acquired in a hundred skirmishes and battles.

So, on this day—June 29, 1966—the spirits of the "Trau Dien" were high. They had been ordered to move north for joint operations with U.S. and ARVN units. Behind them was the tedious, often distasteful duty of riot control in the strife-ridden city of Hue. Now they were leaving the former capital city for operations north of Quang Tri.

The indicated route of motor march would take the Crazy Buffalos north along Route 1. The 1st Vietnamese Army Division intelligence and operations briefing the afternoon before had indicated no particular difficulties; the former "Street Without Joy" had belied its name in recent months. But the battalion commander, a thorough soldier, had developed a cautious and cynical attitude toward "quiet" situations. A march order and a counter-ambush plan was issued, and at his insistence, an ARVN FO team and air cover were provided for the convoy. The Vietnamese Air Force L-19 made its appearance over the column at about 0800, about 5 km north of Hue, shortly after the convoy began the motor march toward the Song O Lau River, some 25 km north.

At first glance, the terrain bordering Route 1 a few hundred meters past the Song O Lau doesn't seem to lend itself to any military use. On the west, low, rolling hills parallel the highway for about 800 meters, ending in a slight military crest at about 200 meters. Beyond this, the terrain is defiladed for about 3,000 meters before rising slowly into the mountain foothills leading into the multi-canopied and rugged jungle merging into Laos. The shallow cross-compartment is covered with knee-high scrub growth that is almost uniform in height.

The critical terrain near Route 1 is the crest of the last or northernmost hill. This hill complex tucks back toward the road at each flank, giving a slight half-bowl effect. The remains of a French fortress are scattered over the last hill.

East of the highway, the terrain slopes away from the road for about 70-100 meters, ending in a scraggly line of short bushes and waste-high grass. Immediately beyond this, the main railroad artery of South Vietnam parallels the highway. The railroad bed, rising from the river, is sunken three or four feet, forming a cut. This entire area adjacent to Route 1 is interdicted here and there with natural, shallow erosion ditches. Concealment is scarce; cover is virtually non-existent.

Sometime on the night of 28 June, the commander of the 802nd Independent Viet Cong battalion, reinforced with a heavy weapons company from the North Vietnamese Army, chose this site along Route 1 for an ambush. He moved his troops into the area in darkness, and he deployed and concealed them methodically and masterfully before first light. He did not trigger his ambush for a jeep carrying two U.S. Army advisors; his troops made no moves when a Popular Force platoon straggled across the bridge and up the road on a routine patrol. Not for this small game had he worked this innocuous terrain into a classic ambush site. He was after bigger game.

When the moment came, he sprang his trap. He misjudged no terrain and he correctly predicted every tactical reaction of his enemy. He only made one miscalculation—and that mistake cost him the better half of his battalion.

Route 1 crosses the Song O Lau on a pontoon bridge next to the sabotaged remains of a former bridge. The lead truck, with Crazy Buffaloes facing outboard along the sides, negotiated the pontoon bridge slowly and then crept up the incline and along the highway in low gear so the other trucks and jeeps could catch up. After all vehicles, including several stragglers, had slowly closed on the leader, the convoy began to pick up speed and had accelerated to about 20 kilometers per hour. The 27-truck convoy, stretched out for about 500 meters, was well within the trap.

Several mortar rounds slammed along the road. Almost simultaneously, 57 mm and 75mm recoilless rifle shells from the hills to the west smashed into the lead truck and three other vehicles, spewing Marines and twisted metal over the road. The convoy stalled, several smoking and burning trucks blocking the highway. It was about 0830.

The Marines in other trucks dismounted quickly and deployed along the shallow ditch to the east, facing to the west where continuing billows of dusty smoke from the backblasts of 57 mm and 75 mm recoilless rifles presaged each shattering impact among the trucks. Enemy small arms fire started in its customary ragged fashion and then settled into an intense, sustained rate. Mortar rounds continued their steady crunch along the highway and erosion area. The volume of fire grew deafening. From the lowest hills nearest the highway, small groups of camouflaged Viet Cong infantry began to move forward by fire and maneuver toward the disabled convoy.

The ambushers had achieved total surprise, as witnessed by the fact that two-dozen civilians, in various modes of transportation, also shared this common impact ground. Their presence added to the confusion of the first minutes, and some were killed in the crossfire. Four water buffalo also died in the initial onslaught.

Within two minutes, it had become terribly clear that this was a big, well-supported ambush designed for the complete annihilation of the 2nd Battalion. It had also become painfully evident to the Marine defenders, as casualties among officers and men alike continued to mount, that this demise would probably occur in these miserably shallow and wide open ditches if something was not done quickly.

The battalion commander, issuing orders rapidly over his radio, directed his companies to dash east, across the 70 to 100 meters of open ground, toward the relative sanctuary offered by the railroad cut. In the near unison, the surviving members of all five companies turned and ran toward the defile.

The CP group, pinned near the center of the ambushed convoy with elements of H & S Company, also moved toward the cut. As the lead elements reach the defile and took cover, the CP group was staggered by a storm of automatic weapons fire. The battalion commander caught one burst full in the chest and fell mortally wounded, along with most of the key personnel in the

The infamous "Street Without Joy" (Road 1), which was the main north-south route from Quang Tri to Hue. Many a French convoy, and French soldiers, suffered heavy losses on this deadly stretch of roadway controlled by the Communists.

command group. Virtually all staff members, including the ARVN FO team, were either killed or wounded in the movement toward the railroad cut.

The Marines who had reached refuge in the cut were now surprised by a well-placed machine gun firing directly down the cut. As this fire started, two companies of well-camouflaged Viet Cong infantry rose from scrub growth 30 meters farther east and attacked on line straight into H&S Company and the remnants of the CP group.

The attack could not be stopped. The Marines fought where they stood. Those in the cut were killed to a man. The previous survivors of the CP group were now added to the casualties, either killed or seriously wounded, and command and control of the battalion vanished with them.

The remainder of H&S Company turned and moved toward the defensive perimeter hastily established about 100 meters to the south by the 2nd and 4th Companies. This move cost H&S Company additional casualties from mines along the railroad cut and tracks.

At this point, the Crazy Buffalo Battalion was no longer a cohesive unit but rather two separated defensive positions battling for survival, without central control. The enemy had accomplished its mission of scattering the battalion and disrupting command and control. They could expect panic among the Marines, with the units dissolving into individuals frantically fleeing to safety. But this was not to be the case for the 2nd Battalion.

To the north, the 1st and 3rd Companies had contracted their lines into a 360-degree, all-around defensive perimeter. These companies were in fairly open terrain and did not have to contend with enemy units physically assaulting their hasty defenses. But the enemy continued to rake the Marine defenders with small arms and recoilless rifle fire from the adjacent hills. The return fire of the defenders was woefully weak compared to the volume of firing facing them. To add to this imbalance, all the enemy mortars shifted their fire from the close combat farther south of the northern position.

Task Force Headquarters: Wha Ho, Vietnam – 12 March 1966. Left to right: Major Tom Campbell, Capt. J.P. Williams, 1st Lt. Roger Groot, and Capt. Paul Slack.

To the south, the 2nd and 4th Companies (with the surviving H&S elements) also had established a defensive perimeter by this time. The fight in this sector had boiled down to a close-in, small arms and grenade engagement with the Viet Cong pushing the attack aggressively. The battalion executive officer was in command of this Marine position, but since nearly all communicators and radiomen had been killed and their radios damaged, assumption of command by a single individual over the two groups was impossible. Even in the early minutes of the fight, radio communications between adjacent units had been difficult and unreliable. Whether this had been caused by enemy jamming efforts or by a communications "dead spot" did not matter a few minutes later—when it counted, radio contact was maintained only with difficulty, and centralization of command did not occur.

At the outset of the ambush, the battalion commander had put in an emergency call for air support. This call had been relayed by the Vietnamese L-19 pilot and was quickly answered. As the events already described were taking place, two U.S.A.F. L-19s had reported on station, and attack sorties were winging their way north from Danang. The L-19s were quickly oriented, and minutes later a flight of four F-4s moved into orbit pattern overhead. A free-bomb zone 200 meters on either side of the road was declared, and the fighter-bombers bored in for the attack.

This prompted the Viet Cong commander to order his units to break contact and withdraw. The enemy engaging the southern perimeter pulled back in good order and commenced a withdrawal to the east. The major enemy units to the west began quitting their positions to withdraw to the west. This withdrawal was accomplished in good order, but their movement over the military crest exposed them to an unopposed volume of fire from the Marine defenders in the north. As the withdrawal commenced, the crews of the recoilless rifles could be clearly seen man–handling their weapons out of position. The entire hill complex became covered with heretofore unseen enemy soldiers, hundreds of them.

In this general withdrawal phase, the enemy commander chose to play one last trump card. He placed in action four 12.5 mm anti-aircraft guns, which had been silent until now. They directly engaged the L-19s and the F-4s moving into attack.

For all purposes, the crippling ambush of the 2nd Battalion was finished. Up to this point, the enemy commander had been total master of the situation. It is here that his only calculated risk, his only mistake, came into play. Facing him, to the west, was more than 3,000 meters of open terrain. There was literally little more than isolated clumps of brush to provide concealment for this entire distance. The enemy troops had no option but to run the gauntlet against the combined fires of quickly converging reaction forces.

The scene, as reported by the aircrews, was one of massed infantry in the open. The L-19s did not even mark the target. The air attack opened with an F-4 expending his full load, in one pass, across the western front of the fleeing enemy lines. This compelled the mass of enemy to swerve right, to the north. The second fighter quickly attacked along this new direction of movement, turning the enemy once more—this time to the east. The target now was an open area approximately 400 meters square with the enemy almost making a circling movement.

Now other friendly forces joined the battle. A reaction company from the U.S. 4th Marines, which had been providing perimeter security for a firing battery supporting a U.S. Marine operation to the north and east, quickly moved by truck across the Song O Lau and up the road, dismounted, and then moved west in pursuit of the smaller group of enemy. Accompanying this U.S. Marine Company was a platoon of Ontos which also turned west after crossing the river.

The Ontos move quickly along the Song O Lau, south of the ambush, and finally arrived at a slightly elevated piece of terrain which proved a clear view of the air attacks. Initially the platoon commander thought he had arrived too late and was observing a friendly unit moving toward him. But upon closer examination with his binoculars, he ordered his weapons to engage. Within seconds, the 106 mm recoilless rifles of his platoon were pounding the enemy ranks.

This added firepower compounded the enemy panic. Friendly prisoners who had been caught up by these units and who later escaped reported that stark terror seemed to grip the enemy troops after the initial counterattack began. Crew-served and individual weapons were abandoned as the enemy sought frantically to escape the trap. About 90 minutes later, another reaction force, comprising two Vietnamese Airborne battalions under the temporary operational control of the 1st ARVN Division, entered the battle by helicopters, setting down about 3 km west of the air and Ontos engagement. This reaction force further closed the trap on the enemy forces.

Meanwhile, the pursuing air and Ontos attacks continued on what was still a lucrative target. By late morning, ARVN infantry units sweeping through the area encountered only scattered enemy survivors, and the entire area from the ambush site to the western foothills was littered with enemy bodies, either singly or in small groups. The ambush force left 326 dead on the field that day.

The two U.S. Marine advisors to the "Trau Dien" battalion had also been caught in the ambush. The senior battalion advisor, after the initial enemy assault opened, joined with the battalion command group and began transmitting an "any station" emergency call, giving position and situation and requesting air support. He was later wounded when the command post group was riddled by enemy fire. The assistant advisor, who had been with the lead elements of the battalion, was able to direct and adjust U.S. Marine artillery fire on the enemy's ridgeline dispositions prior to the arrival of the reaction forces.

The ambush, and the subsequent reaction operations, are both classics of their type. But what of the one miscalculation that cost the Viet Cong commander so heavily? Why did the enemy commander, who had obviously experienced and competent, fail to provide or plan for an egress route for his western and largest contingent? The eastern companies of his force got away without being subjected to any air or artillery fire, because of the cover and concealment offered on that side of the highway beyond the railroad cut.

It can only be conjectured, that the Viet Cong commander was influenced by one or both of two factors. The first is that he greatly misjudged the time required to bring the preponderance of reaction forces and fire to bear on him. He may have felt that his antiaircraft guns would provide enough covering fire for withdrawal, and that this fire, coupled with the fact that the river constituted a natural boundary between the two friendly units, would provide him the necessary time to escape.

The second factor to be considered is that the commander may have been ordered to make the assault regardless of cost. The 2nd Battalion was one of South Vietnam's elite forces and had played a key role in restoring order in Saigon, Danang and Hue during the preceding three months. The National Liberation Front and the Viet Cong had applauded and supported the civil strife resulting from the Buddhist riots of the spring of 1966, particularly those in Hue. In contrast, the 2nd Battalion's efforts to restore order had been forceful and decisive; its enforcement of government regulations had been exacting. So the political and propaganda merits of inflicting a major defeat on the 2nd Battalion may not have been lost on the NFL and Viet Cong leadership.

There is more to this story, however.

The 2nd Battalion was dealt a crippling blow by the ambush. Its loss in officers, trained noncommissioned officers and battle-hardened Marines proved nearly fatal to the battalion. But with the same determination which kept it a disciplined, fighting unit during a period when a frantic retreat would have been readily understandable, the 2nd Battalion turned to the process of rebuilding itself. New officers took up the leadership task, new platoon leaders and squad leaders were found, and incoming recruits were subjected to intensified training.

Within several months, the 2nd Battalion was up to full strength again and ready for combat. When committed to action once more, it proved to be a confidant, competent battalion. The near-annihilation had been overcome and the battalion's staunch defense in the face of overwhelming odds had been converted into unit pride and "Crazy Buffalo" tradition.

Marine Advisor Tom Campbell, Bong Son Qwan area, March '66. Tom retired as a Colonel... he is a lecturer, writer, and historian.

OPERATION LAM SON 719

Marine John G. Miller

To the more wary, or perhaps the more jaundiced, U.S. advisors in South Vietnam, Operation Lam Son 719 in early 1971 appeared to be a snake-bitten venture from the outset. First, there was a problem of high command. As a test of the Vietnamization program, the U.S. plan to maximize South Vietnamese involvement in the war, the Lam Son incursion into Laos carried the highest hopes of both Saigon and Washington. But the commander of the operation, Lieutenant General Hoang Xuan Lam of I Corps, and his staff lacked experience in planning and conducting a mission that involved major units of the Army of the Republic of Vietnam (ARVN) such as the 1st Infantry Division, the 1st Armored Brigade, and a Ranger group augmented by Airborne and Marine units from the National Reserve; each unit was taking the field at division strength for the first time. Even so, the South Vietnamese task force numbered only 16,000 men—half the size of the combined American-Vietnamese force that had launched a cross-border operation into Cambodia a year earlier. To further complicate matters there was no love lost between General Lam and ARVN Marines, who privately referred to him as 'Old Bloody Hands' for the way he would sweep his hands grandly across a battle map while discussing his operational concepts. To the Marines, such bold sweeps would ultimately translate into excessive casualties.

The strategy behind Lam Son 719 called for the creation of a string of helicopter-supported firebases to protect the flanks of a main armored advance along Route 9 from South Vietnam's Khe Sanh Plateau to the principal objective, the village of Tchepone, a point on the Ho Chi Minh Trail lying some 22 km inside Laos. Severing the trail would deny the enemy in South Vietnam vital supplies. Such heavy reliance on helicopters, however, was more appropriate to the flatter country of the Mekong Delta and Cambodia, as both the terrain and the weather became increasingly less hospitable closer to the rugged demilitarized (DMZ) at the seventeenth parallel. In such surroundings, the U.S. advisors would have preferred to attack Tchepone with a near-invulnerable foot column of the ARVN divisions, supported by armor, and then swing either north or south as the opportunity arose. They feared that under the existing strategy, the crucial firebases would be subject to defeat in detail.

Opinions also differed as to the strength of the opposition that the North Vietnamese Army (NVA) could muster against the incursion. To some, the intelligence officers' prediction of a sluggish NVA response to Lam Son 719—one that would be further diluted by a proposed amphibious feint against the North Vietnamese coastal city of Vinh—seemed too optimistic to be taken seriously.

The misgivings of the advisors went unheard during the compartmentalized and tightly guarded planning cycle and, unfortunately, this secrecy did more to isolate the South Vietnamese High Command from reality than to deny essential information to North Vietnamese agents. Thanks to numerous weak spots in South Vietnamese security, the NVA was soon aware of the growing details of the operation on an almost daily basis.

The Marines were designated as the Corps reserve for Lam Son 719, but on D-day, 8 February 1971, none of the division's three brigades had arrived at the Khe Sanh jump-off point. Two were conducting reconnaissance missions in the vicinity of Quang Tri City, also in I Corps, and the third was operating in Cambodia's Neak Luong–Kompong Trach area. By the end of the month, however, all three brigades were at Khe Sanh and the division's command post had been airlifted from Saigon to assume direct operational control in the field for the first time.

Mastering the mechanics of division-level command and control was only part of the problem that the Marines faced. A psychological barrier still existed. The brigade commanders, accustomed to the exercise of absolute authority within their own spheres, were reluctant to accept orders, or even advice, from division staff officers who have less seniority. Consequently, a tradition of semi-independent operations persisted, despite a need for more centralized control.

Early in March, Marine brigades 147 and 258 moved into Laos, and manned firebases Delta and Hotel in order to release troops of the ARVN 1st Division for the final assault on Tchepone. Brigade 369, the only unit remaining in the National Reserve, manned the Laotian border.

Tchepone, by then a deserted, bombed-out village, was occupied briefly by South Vietnamese troops on 9 March. However, earlier plans to sweep southwards had to be abandoned as the NVA was reinforcing its units in the area and was close to achieving a numerical superiority of nearly two-to-one. To make matters worse, even more enemy reinforcements were on the way. The ARVN units, by contrast, were stretched to the limit and additional forces could not be committed to Lam Son 719 without severely weakening their positions in South Vietnam. Furthermore, flying weather was beginning to take a turn for the worse; an ominous portent for the string of firebases still heavily dependent on helicopter support. On 10 March, the South Vietnamese forces were ordered to withdraw.

The withdrawal phase of any military operation is inherently the most dangerous, for as fewer and fewer units are left in contact with the enemy, so they must bear proportionately greater burdens in protecting the flanks and rear of the withdrawing force. This axiom was demon-

Heavily loaded Vietnamese Marines on combat patrol. Marine (center) is carrying a mortar for organic fire support.

strated once again in Lam Son 719, as the string of firebases fell to NVA attacks. The North Vietnamese tactics were uncomplicated: they would first encircle a base to cut off escape and prevent relief by ground units. Next, the encirclement would be tightened, and anti-aircraft weapons would be brought up to shut off aerial resupply. The NVA would go to almost any length to isolate the firebases: American helicopter pilots even saw enemy soldiers lying on their backs beneath the barbed wire that ringed the bases, firing their small arms straight up into aircraft making their final approaches into landings zones. Then, as helicopter losses mounted and the firebase garrisons grew desperately short of food, water, and ammunition, the attackers would wait for a cloudy day, when close support from fixed-wing aircraft would be impossible. At that point, they could bring up their tanks and overrun the position.

Effective air support was the only means available to the South Vietnamese to counter such tactics. For the Vietnamese Marines, this was usually controlled by a pair of U.S. advisors, known as Co-Van My, per battalion, talking to American aircraft overhead. But the congressional mandate that had brought the advisors out of Cambodia on 30 June 1970 was still in effect, and no Co-Van was permitted to accompany his unit into Laos. Somewhere in the chain of command, one feeble concession to reality had been granted, and a single advisor was permitted to be airborne over the division's sector at any given time. This had more cosmetic than real value as an advisor usually had his hands full while working close support for his own battalion. Meeting the simultaneous requirements of six battalions in contact with the enemy, without a man on the ground to mark targets, and to coach high-performance aircraft onto them, was sometimes more than a single advisor could handle.

The pressure on the outnumbered South Vietnamese units intensified steadily during the withdrawal phase. Some managed to return to their homeland in relatively good order. Others did not, and a notorious news photograph of terrified ARVN soldiers clinging to the skids of an evacuation helicopter became an unfortunate and misleading symbol of Lam Son 719 to newspaper readers around the world.

Toward the end of March, the counter-attacking North Vietnamese forces were able to concentrate upon the two Marine brigades in Laos. Two NVA regiments moved in from South Vietnam's A Shau Valley to surround firebase Delta, still defended by Brigade 147. Meanwhile, another North Vietnamese regiment attacked firebase Hotel, pinning down its defenders from Brigade 258. Following the now–familiar pattern, the NVA units next moved ten anti-aircraft guns into the hills surrounding Delta, while hammering the firebase with 130 mm artillery. The noose was drawing tight.

At first light on 21 March, they attacked. The defenders of Delta combined artillery, close air support and a B-52 bomber strike that landed squarely on a North Vietnamese battalion, killing 400 men, to stall the attack. The respite was short–lived, and the North Vietnamese renewed the assault on the following day from positions within the base's defensive perimeter. Brigade 147's casualties were mounting and their supply of ammunition was becoming dangerously low. Darkness was falling on the second day when the NVA forces launched their final attack. By midnight, they had overrun the firebase. The Marines fell back towards the northeast, trying to break through the encircling forces. By noon of the following day, they had established and secured a helicopter-landing zone, to facilitate their evacuation to South Vietnam. Marines who retired from Delta, in other directions found themselves having to escape from the enemy by working their way cross-country towards friendly positions.

Back at Khe Sanh, uneasiness grew steadily as hours when by without the base receiving a word from the stragglers. Khe Sanh had other problems as well: the division's command post, dug in and sandbagged after a few carefree days as a tent city, was falling under heavy attack from 122 mm and 130mm artillery, adjusted by observers from the massive Co Roc escarpment that overlooked the Khe Sanh Plateau. In a typical bit of graveyard humor, U.S. advisors in the hills surrounding Khe Sanh pretended to adjust the North Vietnamese artillery fire on the Co-Van radio network, for the (presumed) amusement of the division-level advisors located within Khe Sanh.

The advisors in Khe Sanh had their own ways of fighting back. One, a son-in-law of the legendary U.S. Marine General, Lewis 'Chesty' Puller, was a veteran of the 1968 Khe Sanh siege. He had saved his old battle maps. When an incoming artillery round landed near the old landing strip, he pulled out his compass and shot a back azimuth towards the estimated source of fire. Then, he raced to the other end of the old airstrip and shot another back azimuth, which happened to intersect with the first one at the same point on the map where a North Vietnamese artillery position had been plotted back in 1968. The advisor's call for counter-battery fire produced a series of spectacular secondary explosions when a great amount of enemy ammunition went up.

Within two days, the Marine stragglers began to return to friendly lines, easing the anxiety at Khe Sanh. By 25 March, after Brigade 258 had conducted an uneventful return by helicopter from firebase Hotel, the casualty figures from the Marine Division were 335 killed in action and 768 wounded, most coming from Brigade147. On the credit side, the initially high missing-in-action total had shrunk to 37, and the returning Marine riflemen were re-equipping, resolutely re-grouping and moving back into the hills to help defend Khe Sanh.

At first, some of the Marines appeared to be 'whipped' by their searing experience, but it became evident that in clawing their way back into Vietnam, they had inflicted at least as much punishment as they had suffered. An enemy radio broadcast named several regiments that would be returning home for a well-deserved 'rest'. Later, these units quietly disappeared from the North Vietnamese order of battle.

The advisors and the Marine leadership approached their shared re-building task with determination. Within a year, these Marines would anchor the defensive line that stopped the North Vietnamese offensive of 1972, and would eventually retake what was left of Quang Tri City.

Accompanying the re-building process was a subtle shift from brigade to division-level thinking. A harbinger of this change appeared shortly after the Marine Division moved from Khe Sanh to the vicinity of Quang Tri. The division's G-3 (operations) officer had flown to one of the brigade command posts, after redrawing boundaries for areas of operation. The brigade commander did not like his new area and, with an almost contemptuous wave of the hand, he told the G-3 to fly back to his headquarters and pick out a better area for his brigade.

The G-3 officer was crestfallen, but his U.S. advisor was seething with frustration. Drawing his opposite number aside, the Co-Van spoke with unusual vehemence, "If you go back to Corps, you will never be a real G-3! You must speak with the authority of the division commander."

Taken aback by this outburst, the G-3 made two calls, using the field telephone. The first was to the division commander, who confirmed what the advisor had said. Next, the G-3 called the contentious brigade commander. With new authority in his voice, he told the senior officer to carry out his orders, as directed, in his assigned area. He would be a real G-3. The South Vietnamese Marines were coming of age as a fighting division.

Lieutenant Colonel De, Commanding Officer 9th Vietnamese Marine Battalion, chats with his US Marine Corps Advisors, Captain Alastair Livingston and Major Paul Carlson, about their involvement in Lam Son-72.

"The battlefield is a lonely place; they are the loneliest people in the world--these advisors in the districts and with ARVN battalions...These men and their courageous brothers–in–arms who daily face the dangers of combat and exact a heavy toll from the enemy who would enslave a people, form a winning team...."

—*General Harold K. Johnson*
Chief of Staff, U.S. Army, 1966

Top News of the Week

The World

South Vietnamese troops pushed into the North Vietnamese-held provincial capital of Quang Tri in northern South Vietnam. Heavy fighting marked the South Vietnamese drive. The North Vietnamese hit Hue, south of Quang Tri, with the biggest artillery barrage since the start of the Communist offensive three months ago.

As South Vietnamese troops push deeper into North Vietnamese-held Quang Tri Province, Gen. Ngo Quang Truong, commander of the attack force, waits with South Vietnamese marines for the start of a helicopter assault.

Left to right: Major General Bui The Lan with General Ngo Quang Truong, 1972.

> "…lives, careers, battles, and the fate of nations have hung on the ability of military leaders to state all the true facts to the best of their knowledge regardless of what effect these facts may have on themselves or others."
>
> —*Samuel Hayes*

Lieutenant Colonel Gerald Turley, Assistant Senior Marine Advisor 1972. Turley was on his second tour in Vietnam when ordered by a U.S. Army General to take charge of all military actions in I Corps when the North Vietnamese launched a full-scale invasion across the DMZ, and elsewhere, with tanks and heavy artillery during the Easter Offensive. His leadership and the willingness of the South Vietnamese to fight and die, successfully stopped this attack. Colonel Turley is the author of The Easter Offensive – The Last American Advisors Vietnam, 1972.

EASTER INVASION 1972

Marines G.H. Turley and M.R. Wells

I Corps was almost peaceful again. Seven years of hard fighting had faded into the past as a feeling of tranquility spread through Quang Tri Province. Highways, long closed, were open and filled with traffic which stimulated the rebirth of a blossoming economy. Marketplaces in Cam Lo, Dong Ha and Quang Tri City, humming with the incessant chatter of bargaining Vietnamese, were heavy with food and wares. Around them, an ugly war was slowly dying. U.S. Marines, from the 3rd Division had been out of country over two years. A battle area once known as "Leatherneck Square," remained only a dim memory. Under President Nixon's Vietnamization plan, the last U.S. Army combat brigade in Northern I Corps was rapidly preparing to stand down. The South Vietnamese were now shouldering the full responsibility for the ground combat role.

In place of 80,000 U.S. troops, which had departed I Corps, stood the fledging 3rd ARVN Division. Reinforced by two brigades of Vietnamese Marines, Regional and Popular Forces the division still totaled less than 9,000 men. The division was headquartered at Ai Tu (Quang Tri) Combat Base, 3 km northwest of Quang Tri City. Thinly spread over 300 square miles were the 3rd ARVN's 2nd, 56th, and 57th Regiments plus Marine Brigades 147 and 258; altogether, a token defense force.

The 57th ARVN Regimental area of operation (AO) extended from Dong Ha, due north to the DMZ and east to the Gulf of Tonkin. The regiment's infantry and artillery battalions were positioned on fire support bases (FSB) Alpha-1, Alpha-2 (Gio Linh) and Alpha-3. All bases fronted the DMZ, 2,000 meters to the north. This regiment, less than six months old, had its headquarters at FSB C-1 midway between Dong Ha and the DMZ. The 2nd ARVN Regiment's AO included combat bases north of Cam Lo, at Alpha-4 (Con Thien), Charlie-2 and Charlie-3. Located at FSB Carroll, and activated a brief 90 days earlier, was the 56th ARVN regiment. This regiment had its infantry units at FSB's Fuller, Khe Gio and Carroll. Collocated at FSB Carroll was a composite artillery group of 22 pieces varying from 105 mm howitzers to 175 mm guns. At an earlier time, the 3rd ARVN Division Commander had developed a plan to periodically rotate his forces through each regimental area of operations. On 30 March 1972, the 56th and 57th Regiments commenced to exchange their AO's. To ensure maximum use of trucks, convoys alternated unit displacements by carrying full loads of troops in both directions. It was anticipated this administrative move could be completed by dusk that same day. The rotation began on schedule and by 1100 approximately 40 percent of each regiment had been relocated. Both regimental headquarters were also in the process of displacing. There was no urgency; the front was calm on this Holy Thursday. The warm spring sun signaled the customary noonday siesta an hour away. At the same time far to the west the 4th Vietnamese Marine Battalion, located on FSB's Sarge and Nui Ba Ho sighted enemy troop movements of platoon and company size. Moments later the 8th Marine Battalion, Bravo Command Group on FSB Holcomb reported enemy ground contact with an estimated company size force. These were the first ground contacts of the 1972 North Vietnamese Easter Invasion.

Precisely at noon, on 30 March, the main body of a North Vietnamese Army, three divisions strong, invaded South Vietnam. Over 45,000 enemy, reinforced by Russian built tanks, SAM missiles, anti-aircraft weapons and long-range artillery blasted a three-pronged attack across the demarcation line (17th Parallel), which partitioned Vietnam as a result of the 1954 Geneva Accord.

The test of Vietnamization had come. Hanoi, by changing its military tactics to those of conventional war backed by sophisticated machines of destruction had caught the 3rd ARVN Division by surprise. Massive attacks by fire shattered the calm over South Vietnam as the three most northern districts underwent precision artillery barrages. Unprecedented, indiscriminate firings by North Vietnamese gunners struck military and civilians alike, forcing 50,000 refugees to the highways fleeing south toward Quang Tri City. Panic prevailed. The question echoed around the world—could the South Vietnamese Army contain the advancing Communist onslaught.

Within the next 24 hours, over 5,000 artillery and rocket rounds struck all twelve of the major combat bases watching the DMZ. The 56th and 57th Regiments caught in the midst of their AO change were paralyzed, unable to react. Heavy T-54 and amphibious PT-76 tanks roared south sending the untried 3rd ARVN Division reeling back. Fire bases A-one, two, three, four, Fuller, Carroll, Mai Loc, Sarge and Nui Ba Ho were all contained under unrelenting artillery barrages.

By 1800 on 30 March, the 4th Vietnamese Marine Battalion troops on Sarge and Nui Ba Ho had received more than 600 rounds of mixed 82 mm mortar, 122 mm and 130 mm artillery fire. The next 36 hours saw the intensity of incoming fire increase even more as low cloud cover throughout the area prevented the use of tactical air support. Intense enemy pressure at Carroll and Mai Loc prevented these bases from replenishing critically low stocks of ammunition. Artillery support for Sarge and Nui Ba Ho dwindled.

Initially Nui Ba Ho received the brunt of the enemy ground attacks and after repeated assaults were beaten back; the firebase was penetrated. As night closed in, hopelessly outnumbered Vietnamese Marines moved to the southeast corner and, unable to defend their position, began to breach the booby-trapped perimeter wire. North Vietnamese soldiers were now intermingled with Marines. Captain Ray L. Smith, USMC, the advisor, threw himself across the final barrier of booby-trapped concertina thus making a human bridge for the last 30 Marines to leave. Nui Ba Ho was the first combat base to fall to the North Vietnamese Easter Invasion.

Individual acts of heroism occurred everywhere across the 3rd ARVN Division front, but the armored momentum and tenacity of the North Vietnamese invasion could not be restrained. ARVN forces fell back.

FSB Sarge had its perimeter penetrated at 0200, 1 April. At 0345, its gallant defenders were forced to evacuate the shattered peak. The battered Marines of the Battalion Alpha Command Group moved off the eastern slope of the perimeter and were immediately engulfed by the night and forest. For the next two days, small groups of the 4th Battalion evaded the enemy and made a march for their lives back to Mai Loc. All radio contact was lost. The unspoken sensation was that the 4th Marine Battalion had been lost forever.

The 7th Marine Battalion, located in Danang as part of the I Corps reserve when the invasion began, was immediately ordered north. Moving by truck, they arrived at Dong Ha that same night. The following morning the 7th Battalion deployed west of Dong Ha toward Cam Lo eventually reaching FSB Mai Loc where they were placed under OPCON of Brigade 147.

Late on the afternoon of 30 March, Brigade 258, consisting

Victory at Quang Tri is recreated with a celebration in Saigon. This campaign increased the prestige of the Vietnamese Marines who were extremely proud of their discipline and fighting ability.

of the 3rd Artillery and 3rd Infantry Battalion, was directed to displace from FSB Nancy to the Dong Ha Combat Base 30 kilometers northwest. The move was completed at 2300. On the 31st, the 3rd Marine Battalion was positioned to provide security along Route 9 and around Dong Ha Combat Base. On 1 April the brigade headquarters was ordered to move back to Ai Tu and assume overall security for the 3rd ARVN Division command post. The 3rd Marine Battalion remained at Dong Ha.

Lieutenant Colonel Dinh, Brigade 258 Commander, arrived at Ai Tu in time to be greeted by an 800-round artillery barrage. The 6th Vietnamese Marine Battalion, which had been on FSB Barbara, had also just arrived and was assuming the perimeter defense of Ai Tu. Due to the increasing enemy artillery attacks on the 3rd ARVN Division command post, it was necessary to displace the division headquarters back to the Citadel in Quang Tri City. U.S. Advisors, fire support coordination personnel and their control facilities remained at Ai Tu (3rd ARVN Division Forward) and became the only Vietnamese command post north of Danang which contained facilities for the control of U.S. supporting arms assets. As such, it quickly became the focal point for the continued effective employment of U.S. supporting arms for the 3rd ARVN Division. For five critical days naval gunfire missions, B-52 Arc Light strikes, tactical air support and Vietnamese fire support coordination were all controlled from within this one bunker.

Below the DMZ, the battle continued to rage. At 1045 hours, 1 April, Con Thien was evacuated. By 1430 hours FSB's Fuller, Khe Gio and Holcomb had all been evacuated. The NVA were seemingly everywhere. Soldiers, civilians and infiltrating NVA artillery observer teams clogged Highway 1 and Route 9. Military control of ARVN units was fragmented and became ineffective. The enemy further compounded the military situation by jamming the radio nets and transmitting contradicting messages over captured ARVN radios. Several aircraft were shot down during the first two days of the invasion. The U.S. activated rescue missions imposed sudden and large area "no fire zones" on all supporting arms thus complicating responsive fire plans. Hastily developed defensive plans faltered, order was lost.

By the morning of the 2nd, South Vietnamese forces were attempting to reposition and establish a new defensive line along the Cam Lo-Cua Viet River. The last two remaining western fire support bases at Carroll and Mai Loc continued to remain under heavy 82 mm mortar and 130 mm artillery fire.

At 0900, a two-pronged North Vietnamese tank column was reported north and northeast of Dong Ha. The main armor thrust was moving on Highway 1, near FSB C-1. The second tank column was traversing the beaches north of the Cua Viet River's mouth. Immediately grasping the gravity of the situation, the Brigade 258 commander ordered the 3rd Vietnamese Marine Battalion to secure a bridge head on the south side of the Dong Ha Bridges. Anti–tank elements of the 6th Marine Battalion were also ordered north to supporting positions. Vietnamese Marines were now totally committed, the 3rd ARVN Division was without a reserve force. Major Binh, commanding the 3rd Battalion, was ordered to "Hold Dong Ha at all costs." Two companies moved across the Dong Ha Combat Base to the bridges. One company took up defensive positions around the main vehicular bridge. The second deployed to the west along Route 9 to include the adjacent abandoned railroad bridge. An NVA flag was flying from the northern girder of the railroad bridge as the Marines took up hasty fighting positions. Armed with only hand-held M-72 anti-tank weapons, a small force of Marines dug in and prepared to halt the first major NVA tank and infantry assault of the Vietnam War.

Refugees and ARVN stragglers were still streaming south across the main bridge. Population control was becoming a major problem.

As the 3rd Battalion's command element arrived at the bridge, the enemy unleashed a devastating 45-minute artillery attack which precluded any troop movements south of the river. At 1020 the enemy armored column, on Highway 1 was identified as 20 PT-76 and T-54 tanks. PT-76 tanks were also seen traveling south along the beaches. Naval gunfire was brought to bear on both columns. Four columns of black smoke along the beach gave testimony to the ships accurate gunfire.

Along Highway 1, the skies cleared and Vietnamese A-1 aircraft bombed and strafed the Russian tanks, destroying 11. One aircraft was hit by anti-aircraft fire forcing the pilot to bail out. Forces on both sides of the river stopped firing and watched as the parachute drifted to earth. Winds carried the pilot away from the Marines and to certain capture north of the bridge.

As a last desperate measure, an order was issued to destroy the Dong Ha Bridges. At approximately 1115, the lead enemy tank moved on the abutment on the north side of the Cua Viet. Marines took it under fire and struck it once with an M-72 anti-tank round. The tank, partially disabled, backed off and moved into a firing position north of the bridges. The U.S. Advisor, 3rd Marine Battalion began to strategically emplace 500 pounds of assorted explosives diagonally across the spans of the roadways. Under continuous fire by the swelling enemy infantry and tank forces, Captain John W. Ripley, USMC miraculously moved unscratched through the intense enemy fire to place the demolitions. After two hours of preparations, the explosives were charged and at 1630, Captain Ripley sent both bridges crashing into the Cua Viet River.

Stopped at the Dong Ha Bridges, the enemy armored columns turned west toward the Cam Lo bridge complex. Accurate guns from USS *Bachanian*, *Strauss* and *Weddell* rendered these enemy movements ineffective. Throughout the night, offshore guns rained hundreds of shells upon the enemy. "Danger close" targets within 300 meters of the Vietnamese Marines were common fire missions.

For three days, FSB Carroll, with its 22 artillery pieces, had been under constant artillery attack. By 1400, 2 April, enemy ground forces had moved within small arms range of the perimeter. At 1430, an emergency radio appeal from the U.S. Army advisor, 56th Regiment, requested extraction because his ARVN counterpart had elected to surrender. Before any action could be taken at division level, an unknown CH-47 pilot, participating in the last resupply mission to Mai Loc, 3,000 meters to the south, took it upon himself to extract the advisory team. At 1440, a white flag was raised over FSB Carroll and 1,500 ARVN soldiers were lost to the invaders. The sudden lull of enemy artillery gave mute testimony to the fact that the largest concentration of ARVN artillery in I Corps was lost to the North Vietnamese. This unique capitulation psychologically crushed the flickering hopes of many South Vietnamese units fighting across the northern front.

As the sun was setting on this war-torn day, there were two brief moments of

Enlisted members of the 6th Marine Battalion celebrate the 1972, Victory of Quang Tri; the 6th battalion had fought dauntless in the defense of Quang Tri Province and was the spearhead of the Marine assault that retook the Citadel in Quang Tri City in September, 1972.

joy. The 4th Marine Battalion Alpha Group from FB Sarge, with Major Walter E. Boomer, USMC, the battalion's Senior Advisor, had made contact with an aerial observer who guided them back to Mai Loc. Several hours later, at 1745, the 30 survivors of the 4th's Bravo Group from the siege on Nui Ba Ho passed quietly through the gate and rejoined their battalion. The 4th Marine Battalion was now accounted for.

FSB Mai Loc was next as the enemy artillery attacks became more intensive. Remaining radio antennas were shot away and direct communications with the 3rd ARVN Division was lost. Artillery ammunition was down to several hundred rounds with little chance of replenishment. At 1815, Lieutenant Colonel Bao, Brigade 147's commander, made the decision to abandon Mai Loc and march to Dong Ha. When the artillery storage bins were depleted and the last artillery round had been fired, incendiary grenades were placed in the tubes making all ten guns useless to the enemy. Around 1900, with the 200 survivors from the 4th Battalion leading the way, the brigade column moved out under the cover of darkness. Hampered by rain showers, harassed by the enemy guns, the column moved east. The brigade became separated while traversing several precarious stream crossings; however, by 0500 the next morning all units were again linked up. Later that morning the column reached Highway 1, near Dong Ha, turned south and reached Ai Tu at 1800 on 3 April. As the haggard and near exhausted Marines joined at the Brigade 258 command post, weary eyes became misty as comrades greeted each other. The familiar faces of over 300 Vietnamese Marines were gone forever but the brigades were together at last and this gave them the needed strength for the battles ahead.

During the first 78 hours of the Easter Invasion, all major combat bases north and west of Dong Ha had fallen to the NVA invaders. South Vietnamese forces had lost 53 artillery pieces and several thousand soldiers were missing or dead. Whole ARVN units were unlocated. FSB's Pedro, Ai Tu, and Dong Ha Combat Base were the only remaining ARVN strong points north of Quang Tri. Most important, however, the main North Vietnamese invasion thrust was halted and the Communist army's time schedule for seizing Quang Tri City within seven days was disrupted. Vietnamese Marines paid a heavy price, but in doing so bought their government precious time. Time to reposition its forces, time to consolidate, time to act.

The period 3 to 8 April found the South Vietnamese forces maneuvering and strengthening positions around Quang Tri City while the 3rd Marine Battalion repulsed repeated enemy attempts to cross the Cua Viet River at Dong Ha. On 3 April, the Republic's Joint General Staff ordered the Marine Division headquarters and the remnants of the brigade airlifted to the battle area. Division headquarters moved into the Hue Citadel while Brigade 369 set up and a new AO around FSB's Nancy and Jane. At this time, the Commandant of Marines had not received operational control of the full Division as Brigades 147 and 258 were still OPCON to the 3rd ARVN Division.

Shortly after midnight on 9 April, the NVA massed their artillery and began shelling Ai Tu with 130 mm guns. The heavy pounding continued throughout the night. Just before dawn, the 6th Marine Battalion around FSB Pedro reported heavy ground contact. And 0645 first two, then seven and finally sixteen enemy tanks supported with two battalions of infantry advanced on the fire support base. Marine artillery batteries quickly brought accurate fire to bear on the enemy, stalling the infantry attack. At 0715, several enemy tanks advanced, with two T-54s breaching the perimeter. These immediately began crushing all bunkers as the few Marines within the wire withdrew toward Ai Tu. A nearby platoon outpost was overrun and all Marines were killed by gunfire or crushing tank actions. The other T-54's held their positions around Pedro, waiting for their infantry to move up. When the T-54's had completed their destruction, they moved on toward Ai Tu. The 6th Battalion commander had his OP on a small knoll. The two tanks maneuvered toward it. The lead tank struck an anti–tank mine and was disabled. The second moved around his burning mate and continued on to within 50 meters of the 6th's Command Group. The tank stopped, rotated its main gun but did not fire.

Earlier when the first report of an impending tank and infantry attack had been received at Brigade 258, Lieutenant Colonel Dinh began assembling a reaction force. The lead ARVN M-48 tank of the reaction force moved into a firing position just as the enemy T-54 ground to a halt at the 6th's OP. A brief tank battle ensued and the enemy tank was destroyed. Approximately 30 minutes later, the 6th was reinforced by two infantry companies of the 1st Battalion and an ARVN tank and APC armor force of 20 vehicles. A counterattack was launched toward Pedro. As this force deployed a Vietnamese Air Force flight of four A-1 aircraft came on station. This Vietnamese air ground team began to systematically destroy the enemy. The heavy bombardments from Marine 105 mm howitzers force the enemy infantry to abandon the area and withdraw toward the Ba Long Valley. Within two hours 13 of 16 T-54 tanks had been destroyed by mines, tank fire, air strikes and Marine Infantry weapons. Of the remaining three, one withdrew; two were deserted by their crews during the battle. Both captured tanks were proudly driven by Marines back to Ai Tu as war trophies.

The first enemy tank-infantry assault on Pedro was repulsed with the enemy leaving 157 dead on the battlefield. Succeeding enemy attacks came on 10 and 11 April, again the enemy was beaten back with 211 dead NVA left behind. Captured documents later revealed the enemy had launched an infantry regiment and a tank battalion against the Marine Western Front. Their mission was to take both Pedro and Ai Tu and attack the southern flank of the Dong Ha defenses. This three-day battle accounted for the defeat of a major drive to bisect the vital Quang Tri defensive line, which would have destroyed the remaining effectiveness of the 3rd ARVN Division's northern front. More significantly, however, this battle allowed Marine infantry units to discover that they could meet and defeat Russian armor with their organic anti-tank weapons. Russian armor had lost its psychological shock effect on the Vietnamese Marines.

The invading North Vietnamese divisions continued to press their attacks toward Quang Tri City with enemy armor and infantry forces using the Cam Lo Bridge as their primary crossing point. Once south of the Cam Lo-Cua Viet River, NVA units moved on Dong Ha from the west. Other enemy forces moved south, passing FSB Carroll and Mai Loc, on toward Route 557 and FSB Pedro.

On 23 April, Brigade 147, with 4th and 8th Infantry and the 2nd Artillery Battalion returned to Ai Tu from a rest and refitting period in Hue. Brigade 258 deployed to Hue. The 1st Battalion remained at FSB Pedro and changed OPCON to Brigade 147.

At that time, the 4th and 5th Ranger Groups and the 57th ARVN Regiment were located to the north of Ai Tu and around Dong Ha. On the southern flank of the 1st Marines, stood elements of the 2nd ARVN Regiment. The Second's AO extended south from Ai Tu to the Thach Han River and east to Highway 1. Across the Thach Han on the south bank was the 1st Ranger Group.

During the night of 26 April the 3rd ARVN Division issued a warning of an impending attack by the 304th NVA Division. At 0630, a red double star cluster signaled the enemy attack. All ground attacks were launched under the protective cover of intensive artillery fires. The 1st Battalion, which was now positioned 2-3000 meters south of Ai Tu, also came under a heavy 82 mm mortar attack. The battalion beat back two ground attacks. The 8th Battalion had little ground contact across their front at this time, but discovered enemy in their rear area that was to have been secured by an ARVN battalion. During the day, both the 1st and 8th Battalions repulsed tank and infantry attacks, destroying 12 Russian tanks in the process. At dusk, the Marine defense line was straightened as the 1st and 8th were pulled back to within one to two km of Ai Tu. Shortly after dark, enemy artillery fire struck an ammunition dump; most of the stocks were destroyed.

By 28 April the enemy pressure on the Ranger Groups in the Dong Ha area caused all ARVN forces north of Ai Tu to fall back along Highway 1 toward Quang Tri. By nightfall, the Ranger's defensive line was tied in with the 8th Marine Battalion at Ai Tu, and eastward to the river. The 57th ARVN Regiment, in full route, retreated through this defensive line into Quang Tri City. The 2nd ARVN Regiment still held the line southwest of the Quang Tri bridges.

At 0200 on 29 April, the enemy launched a tank-infantry attack around the south end of the Marine minefield on the 2nd ARVN's front along the Thach Han. The attack rolled up the southern flank of the ARVN forces on the west side of the river and penetrated up to the Quang Tri bridges. U.S. tac-air was called in and, working under flares, destroyed three of the enemy tanks. By morning, enemy forces remained in control of the west side of the Quang Tri bridges. Two companies of the 7th Battalion, which had arrived at Ai Tu the night before, reopened the highway to the city by killing 12 NVA in the bridges' west defensive bunkers.

Throughout the day, the defensive situation across the river from Quang Tri City deteriorated. Late that afternoon the Ai Tu ammunition dump was again hit by artillery and the remaining stocks went up in flames. Ammunition for the Marine howitzers became critical as the battalion's guns had less than 1,000 rounds on position.

The NVA continued to exert pressure on Ai Tu. The Ranger Group holding at the east of the 8th Marine Battalion fell back and withdrew into Quang Tri City. Brigade 147 was now almost encircled. At noon on 30 April, the 3rd ARVN Division ordered the Marines to withdraw from Ai Tu and return to the Citadel to provide a defensive force around the city. The withdrawal plan called for the brigade headquarters and the 2nd Artillery Battalion to depart first. Followed by the 1st Battalion; the 8th would follow in trace from the western flank. The 4th Battalion would close the column as the rear guard.

The plan was executed smoothly, with the exception of the 18 artillery pieces and their prime movers. As the Marine brigade was moving on the city, ARVN engineers prematurely destroyed both bridges over the Thach Han River. Attempts were made to tow the howitzers across at a fording site, but due to a soft bottom and currents, this failed. Thus, it was necessary to disable and destroy the howitzers and 22 prime movers. The infantry battalions crossed the river and took up defensive positions around the city as Brigade 147 set up its command post beside the Citadel walls.

At 1215, 1 May, the 3rd ARVN Division advised all units in Quang Tri that the city would undergo a 10,000-round artillery barrage starting at 1700. Military units were ordered to evacuate the city. No orderly withdrawal plan was promulgated. The 27 maneuver battalions under the OPCON of the 3rd ARVN Division were released to fend for themselves. During the afternoon three CH-54 helicopters landed at the Citadel and extracted the ARVN division staff and their U.S. advisors. The last remaining shreds of unity dissipated. The strain and shock of 30 days conventional warfare on ill prepared troops had unraveled the already thin fabric of unit discipline and effectiveness. A frightened mass of humanity moved like a rampant tidal wave onto Highway 1, and south toward Hue, 50 kilometers away. Highway 1, south of Quang Tri, was interdicted by enemy artillery and had been periodically closed by enemy infantry units since 29 April. The roadway was one of incredible destruction. Burning vehicles of all types, trucks, armored vehicles, civilian buses and cars filled the highway forcing all traffic off the road to the east. Tracked vehicles explored cross-country routes as hundreds of civilians were subjected to enemy artillery barrages. Marine Brigade 147, which had its USMC advisors and retained its unity, moved out of the city at 1430. The column was composed of over 30 armored vehicles and four Marine battalions. As the brigade moved south, it was joined by large numbers of ARVN soldiers and civilians. As dusk fell, the column was halted by an estimated NVA regiment just west of Hai Lang. In addition, the Marine column had become so fragmented by intermingling civilians and ARVN stragglers that effective unit control became difficult.

By late afternoon on 2 May, the carnage was complete. The number of civilians killed fleeing Quang Tri Province will never be known, but estimates place it in the thousands. Somehow, several ARVN units and Marine Brigade 147 managed to maintain some order in the midst of hysteria and fought their way to a new Marine defense line.

Marine Brigade 369's defensive lines had been located to the south of Hai Lang along the O'Khe and My Chanh Rivers since deploying north from Saigon. The two bridges crossing these rivers along Highway 1 had to be held if the withdrawing troop and civilians were to successfully move south. On 2 May, a pre-dawn, hour-long, intensive enemy artillery barrage struck the two bridge sites. At first light, elements of an NVA regiment supported by 18 tanks assaulted the O'Khe Bridge area, held by the 9th Marine Battalion. The battle raged through the morning hours and although five tanks penetrated the defensive perimeter, all were destroyed. The enemy, unable to break through, left 17 burning tanks along with several hundred dead infantry on the battlefield. By dusk, Highway 1 north of the O'Khe was void of movement as the

Members of the 6th VNMC Battalion raise their nation's flag over the west gate of the Citadel at Quang Tri City. This was a proud moment for the South Vietnamese people and for the Marines, the culmination of seven weeks of fanatical fighting where one of every five Marines had become a combat casualty. The flag was raised at 1200 hrs. on 16 September, 1972.

enemy closed off all routes of escape. Brigade 369, commanded by Colonel Chung, had completed its mission as a rear guard force and withdrew south of the My Chanh, and redeployed.

The My Chanh Line And Counter-Offensive

As darkness fell on 2 May, South Vietnam's future looked bleak. Near Saigon, there were NVA tanks in An Loc; west of Hue FSB Bastogne had just fallen and to the north all of Quang Tri Province had been lost. The invaders had declared Quang Tri City their Provincial Capital in the south. There was a national atmosphere of desperation, yet a prevailing feeling of grim determination to drive out the Communists. The South Vietnamese Government responded with changes in the military command structure and a new Order of the Day – there would be no further withdrawals. The full test of Vietnamization had come. For Marines, the My Chanh Line would be their decisive battlefield.

After Brigade 147 withdrew past the My Chanh River, it returned to Hue for rest, replacements and refitting. All three Marine brigades and the three artillery battalions had experienced losses of men and equipment during the first five weeks of the invasion. Material combat losses were quickly identified and through the U.S. advisory channels requests for replacements were transmitted to HQMC. In less than 30 days, over 80 percent of the initial equipment losses had been replaced. Trucks flown from Okinawa were hitched to 105 mm howitzers airlifted from Barstow, California and rushed north to the war zone. Every C-141 or C-5A that landed at Danang Air Base demonstrated that although the U.S. Marines

USMC Advisors: Major Stanley Pratt and Captain Wayne Rollings.

were out of the country, they were dedicated to providing full logistical support to the Vietnamese Marines through their most trying period. It was an overwhelming confirmation, and did much to rekindle the spirits of Marines along the My Chanh.

On 4 May, President Thieu appointed Lieutenant General Khanh to the Joint General Staff as assistant for operations. This marked the first time a Vietnamese Marine officer had ever held such a high military office. Colonel Bui The Lan, General Khanh's deputy, was appointed as the new Commandant of Vietnamese Marines.

For the first time since the Easter Invasion began the Marines were assigned their own division area of operations. Their battle line was the northern front, extending from the Gulf of Tonkin on the east, 18 km westward, across Highway 1, and into the foothills. Five infantry battalions were initially positioned along the My Chanh Line. As they were digging in, North Vietnamese units spirited by fresh successes at Ai Tu and Quang Tri City began to probe the line.

On 5 May, Brigade 258 moved forward from Hue to Phong Dien and assumed responsibility of the western half of the division's My Chanh line. On 12 May, Brigade 369 was repositioned on the east flank. At the same time, the NVA was building up its forces for an all out attack on the ancient capital of Hue.

Colonel Lan and Colonel Joshua W. Dorsey III, USMC, Senior Advisor, began to develop plans for putting the Marine Division on the offensive. Under the planning guidance of its Commandant, an immediate counter offensive by Vietnamese Marine across the division front was begun. As an initial step a helicopter assault would be made into the Hai Lang Village area. Utilizing U.S. Marine Corps helicopter assets from the 9th Marine Amphibious Brigade, two Vietnamese infantry battalions were heli-lifted into adjoining landing zones around Hai Lang. One CH-53 was lost to enemy ground fire. The enemy was tactically surprised with over 240 NVA killed by the assaulting Marines and their supporting arms.

The North Vietnamese, momentarily set back by the vertical assault in their rear, responded with a major armor and infantry attack. On 21 May, the NVA moved his forces south on Route 555 and crossed the My Chanh, striking into Brigade 369's AO. Hearing the armor approaching, regional forces along the line fell back, allowing the enemy to almost encircle the 3rd and 9th Battalions. Both units were forced to withdraw, but after intense fighting that lasted throughout the day the Marines had reestablished their defense line back on the My Chanh River. Casualties among the Marines were high, but the enemy suffered heavier losses including the destruction of seven PT-76 and T-54 tanks.

At 0100, on 22 May the 3rd Battalion was again attacked by a large infantry force accompanied by 22-25 tanks. The 3rd Battalion destroyed eight tanks by artillery and M-72's before being overrun by numerically superior forces. The enemy force continued his penetration and moved on Brigade 369's command post, attacking at first light. Five of the enemy's armored vehicles were stopped within 400 meters of the brigade CP. An artillery battery, 200 meters further south literally bore-sighted one gun to stop a PT-76 tank at 140 meters from the battery position. Also, the newly introduced TOW guided missile system destroyed a PT-76 tank with the first round ever fired in combat. Vietnamese Marines, observing the TOW missile glance off a radio antenna, change its deflected course, stopped shooting and cheered as the Russian tank was enveloped in flames. The armored attack was finally repulsed, as 10 tanks and APC's were destroyed. At 0930, the 8th Battalion conducted a counterattack that broke the infantry assault. The enemy fled leaving their dead and wounded behind them. For the NVA the cost was extremely high and nothing was gained. The My Chanh Line was restored by nightfall.

Even as this attack was under way, another counter-offensive operation was being planned. On 23 May, the 7th Marine Battalion was trucked to Tan My, where they boarded U.S. Navy landing craft and embarked aboard ships of the 7th Fleet. Early the next morning the Marine Division conducted a combination amphibious landing and heliborne assault in the Wunder Beach area of Quang Tri Province. The operation, Song Than 6-72, was conducted by Brigade 147 and required close coordination with the 9th MAB, U.S. Navy amphibious shipping, naval gunfire support and B-52 arc-light strikes. Colonel Lan, his G-3 operations officer Lieutenant Colonel Ky, and a small staff coordinated their multi-assault force from on board the CCL-19, Blue Ridge. In many ways, it was a history-making event, as the Vietnamese Marine Corps planned and executed its first assault from the sea. A B-52 arc-light strike thundered across the beach area just as the leading wave of LVTs approached the 2,000-meter offshore mark. Shortly thereafter, the 7th Marine Battalion moved ashore in two waves of 40 amphibious tractors and landed under enemy 82 mm mortar fire. The beachhead was seized. As the USMC tractors turned and went back to sea, the Vietnamese

Marines moved over the sand dunes out of sight. An hour later, again following B-52 strikes, and 6th and 4th Infantry Battalions aboard USMC helicopters were lifted into two landing zones near the junction of Routes 555 and 602. Both battalions landed on time and seized initial objectives against light resistance. For the second time in a month, a major offensive operation had been successfully executed by the Marine Division. The North Vietnamese Army had suddenly discovered its sea flank was vulnerable to the varied tactics of the Marines. Song Than 6-72 ended on 31 May, as all battalions returned to the My Chanh Line.

At 0530 on 25 May, the NVA switched back to the western flank of the Marine Division's AO and launched attacks at Brigade 258's western units. For three consecutive days, the enemy infantry deployed in their daylight attacks prematurely allowing artillery and other friendly supporting arms to be employed with excellent results. Early on the 26th, the 1st Regiment received its heaviest attack as a reinforced enemy battalion was committed to breaking the My Chanh Line. One element of the enemy force almost succeeded in reaching the battalion command post. Ultimately, the attack failed, for by mid-morning, the NVA forces had broken contact, leaving over 200 enemy bodies on the battlefield and stacked around the battalion CP. Two weeks of continuous fighting and heavy losses caused the 66th and 88th NVA Regiments to temporarily retire from the battle area. During May, over 2,900 enemy had been killed, 1,080 weapons captured and 64 armored vehicles destroyed or captured.

The month began with chaos above My Chanh, but ended with a strong northern front anchored by the Vietnamese Marine Division. The My Chanh Line had been subjected to tremendous pressures and although it bent at times, it was never broken. This was due to responsive supporting arms fire plans, excellent small unit leadership and the courage and tenacity of individual Vietnamese Marines. It was a good month for Marines. On 28 May, on the Emperor's Walkway in front of the Old Imperial Palace of the ancient capital of Hue Citadel, President Thieu personally promoted Colonel Lan to brigadier general.

During June, the Vietnamese Marines seized the initiative and began a series of limited offensive operations. The first week there was little ground action. On 8 June, Song Than 8-72 was launched as all brigades advanced north from the My Chanh Line. The Marines, moving forward behind a well-coordinated fire support plan of B-52 strikes, tac-air, naval gunfire and artillery, encountered the heaviest resistance along the coast and Route 555. The operation ended successfully with all brigades having a foothold in southern Quang Tri Province. The Marines lost only nine men while accounting for over 230 enemy killed, 102 weapons and seven tanks or APC's destroyed.

With South Vietnamese forces north of the My Chanh River, ARVN engineers constructed pontoon bridges so armored vehicles could cross back into Quang Tri Province and support the attacking infantry. The tide of battle was slowly, but definitely, turning in favor of the South Vietnamese forces. Another Marine operation, Song Than 8A-72, began on 18 June. The 6th and 7th Battalions move northwest paralleling the beach. The 7th met only light resistance along the coast. Again, the heaviest resistance was encountered along Route 555; and roadway more commonly known to U.S. Marines as "Triple Nickel." Enemy tanks and infantry counter-attacks against the 6th Battalion were ineffectual and

Captain Bill Wischmeyer with the 6th VNMC Battalion, on an outpost that had withstood several enemy assaults.

poorly coordinated, as the NVA still had not been able to organize its armor and infantry units into any semblance of a team effort. With each sighting of tanks, Marine artillery was quick to bring its guns to bear on the enemy armor. (Both Chinese armored personnel carriers and Russian tanks are manufactured with their gasoline tanks on the outside of the vehicle; therefore, it is not necessary to achieve a direct hit to disable or set them on fire.) Marine artillery learned to mass its fires on enemy armor and to exploit this basic weakness.

By 27 June, the Marine Division had pushed the NVA back four km from the My Chanh River. Song Than 8A-72 was completed with 761 enemy killed and eight more tanks destroyed.

June ended with the Vietnamese Marine Corps at its peak combat strength. The infantry battalions were at their highest level ever. In addition, the VNMC recruit training center was operating at maximum capacity, and Marine recruiters had men waiting to enter the Corps. The division's logistical posture was also excellent; almost all the earlier combat losses had been replaced.

I Corps counter-offensive, Song Than 9-72, with the mission of destroying the North Vietnamese Army and recapturing Quang Tri City, began on 28 June. This was a coordinated two-division attack with the Marines operating generally between the coast and Highway 1. The airborne division maneuvered from the Marines left flank west to the Anamite foothills. Quang Tri City was included in the airborne division's AO. Song Than 9-72 was in full swing as the month ended, and the NVA were on the defensive in all sectors of the I Corps front. During June, 1,515 enemy were killed, 18 armored vehicles were destroyed. The captured column registered 15 POW's, four armored vehicles and 550 weapons. Slightly over 150 Vietnamese Marines lost their lives during June.

Throughout July, the Marines remained in heavy contact, as 1,880 enemy were killed in action. Enemy material losses were equally heavy as Marines destroyed or captured 51 armored vehicles, seven Russian 37 mm antiaircraft guns, four artillery pieces, a 20-ton ammunition dump and over 1,200 individual weapons.

On the morning of 11 July, the 1st Vietnamese Marine Battalion was heli-lifted by 28 USMC helicopters into a landing zone 2,000 meters directly north of Quang Tri City. Its mission was to block Route 560 and prevent the enemy from re-supplying his units in the Citadel. U.S. Army Air Calvary gunships led the helicopter waves into the landing zone. Even though the objective area had been struck by extensive preparatory fires, most of the helicopters were hit by enemy ground fire. One CH-53 was struck by an SA-7 heat seeking missile, causing it to burst into flames, killing a full load of Vietnamese Marines. To secure his tenuous position, Major Hoa, the battalion commander, personally led his battalion in an assault against the well-entrenched enemy. Two more trench lines had to be seized before the perimeter was secure. A USMC naval gunfire spot team officer was hit almost immediately after leaving a helicopter. Captain Lawrence H., Livingston, USMC, the battalion advisor, left his position beside Major Hoa and moved across the fire swept rice paddies to carry the wounded lieutenant to safety. Corporal Jose F. Hernandez, USMC, the spot team radio operator, also braved enemy fire to help wounded Vietnamese Marines to safety. He then commenced to call in naval gunfire missions to prevent the NVA from reinforcing. Over 100 Marines lay wounded, but medical evacuation was impossible as the enemy had inter-dicted the LZ with artillery, mortar and antiaircraft fire. Three days of heavy fighting were required to permanently close off the enemy's main supply route into Quang Tri City. With the line secure, the first medevac's were finally accomplished on the evening of 14 July.

On 22 July, another heliborne assault was executed along the coastline about 10 kilometers northeast of Quang Tri City. Again, USMC helicopters with the 5th Vietnamese Marine battalion, landed behind the NVA's main line of resistance. No planes were hit and only moderate contact was encountered in the landing zone. As events turned out this was the last U.S. Marine Corps-supported heliborne operation of the Vietnam War.

The airborne division, keeping abreast on the left flank of the Marines, entered Quang Tri City in early July. But, exhausted and depleted from previous battles at An Loc and the Central Highlands, they could not recapture the city. After several weeks of heavy casualties and limited progress by the paratroopers, the Marine Division was ordered to relieve the airborne division and retake Quang Tri City. Brigade 258 received the mission and the in-place relief was completed at 2130, 27 July. Prior to relief, the nearest airborne unit was still 200 meters from the Citadel walls. The last four days of July were devoted to extensive artillery preparation fires on the city, while the enemy countered with substantially increased artillery of its own.

Throughout August, the enemy kept heavy pressure on Brigade 147, just north of the city, as the brigade continued to block Route 560. All enemy supplies entering the city now had to be ferried across the Thach Han River. During the month, Brigade 147 was in contact with all 3 regiments of the 325th NVA Division, as well as the 27th Independent Regiment. August also found Brigade 258's four infantry battalions devoted to heavy house-to-house fighting around the Citadel. The 3rd Battalion was attacking from the northeast, the 9th and 6th from the southeast and the 1st from the southwest. The enemy kept an almost continuous artillery and mortar barrage falling on the Marine battalions. Over 720 attacks by fire, exceeding 50,000 rounds, struck friendly positions in and around the city. While little progress was gained on the ground, the Vietnamese Marine Corps inflicted heavy casualties in some of the hardest fighting of the war. There were 2,322 enemy killed during the month. However, after 30 days of slow progress, it was apparent that more combat power would be needed to wrest the city from elements of three NVA regiments. Thus, on 8 September, the 1st Ranger group's three battalions relieved Brigade 147 of its blocking positions north of the city. This enabled General Lan to employ two Marine brigades in a direct assault on Quang Tri City. Brigade 258, with its four battalions, continued its attack from the south and southwest. Brigade 147, with the 3rd and 7th Battalions, attacked from the northeast. On 9 September, the final assault on Quang Tri City began. Intensive artillery and tactical air preparations fire were placed on the Citadel and adjacent parts of the city. Lieutenant Colonel Tung, commanding officer, 6th Marine Battalion, set up his forward command post 300 meters south of the southeast corner of the Citadel and there, observing through a small hole in the second floor wall, the USMC Advisor coordinated and adjusted over 200 sorties of tac-air on the Citadel.

During the night of 9-10 September, a small squad of Marines from the 6th Battalion slipped in and out of the Citadel. Early on the 11th, a platoon from the 6th moved over the southeast corner of the wall. The enemy continued to resist fanatically, but the massive supporting arms fires and air strikes, steadily crushed its will to fight. At dawn on 15 September, the 3rd Battalion moved over the northeast corner and joined with the 6th Battalion to clear the east wall of the ancient fortress. Together, they turned west and began to clear the 500 meter-square Citadel. Marines of these battalions, unable to hold back their exuberance, shouted with joy as they swept across the rubble and seized the western wall of the Citadel. At 1700, the Citadel was cleared and in complete control of the Marines. All other enemy resistance collapsed. Quang Tri City was returned to RVN control.

In seven weeks of fanatical fighting, under the unrelenting shelling of enemy artillery and mortars, one of every five Marines had become a combat casualty. South Vietnamese Marines had climbed their mountain. At 1200, 16 September, they raised their nation's scarlet and gold flag over the western gate of the Quang Tri Citadel and, in so doing, gave signal to the world that the South Vietnamese could more than stop the aggressors, they could soundly defeat them. Vietnamese Marines, short in stature, rich in courage, and full of determination, stood tall in the eyes of all Marines.

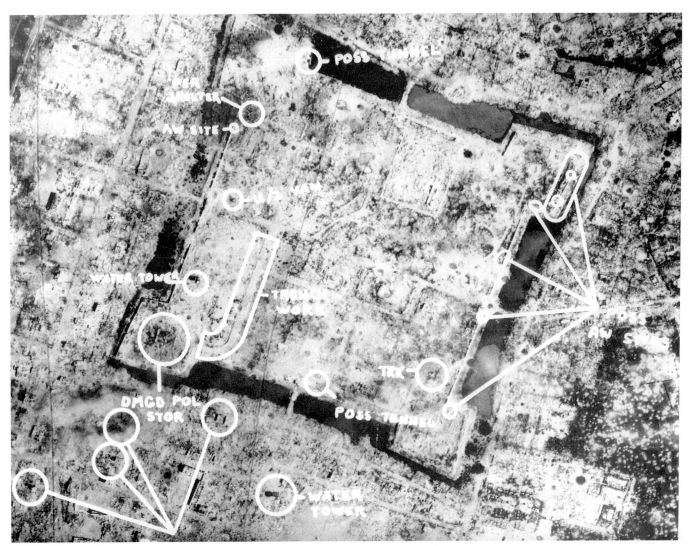

Air photograph of the Quang Tri Citadel, 12 August 1972. Suspected enemy positions are annotated.

Brigadier General Bui The Lan, Commandant of the Vietnamese Marine Corps (left), Colonel Joshua Dorsey, the last senior Marine Advisor (center), and Brigadier General Edward J. Miller, Commanding General 9th Marine Amphibious Brigade (right) discuss the Vietnamese tactical area of responsibility at General Lan's Headquarters at Huong Dien; the Marine Division had moved its forward command post from Hue City to this coastal village north of Hue. Note General Lan's nametape, "Laan" was an aid for pronounciation for the benefit of the Americans. 1972.

With maps in hand, Captain John W. O'Donnell, USMC, Senior Advisor to the VNMC's 1st Battalion, and Captain Hien, battalion operations officer, discuss their location and movement of the battalion during a search and destroy operation in rain-drenched Quang Tri Province. The operation was conducted in an area covered by snow-white sand during midwinter in the northern province.

VNMC Marines preparing for an operation.

Vietnamese Marines returning from a combat patrol – Hue, 1967.

Vietnamese Marines assemble at the rear of a U.S. Marine Corps helicopter to off-load supplies for their units. Resupply items include radio batteries, rice and ammunition.

RIPLEY AT THE BRIDGE:
DONG HA, SOUTH VIETNAM
2 APRIL 1972

Marine Charles D. Melson

There were few Americans in combat in Southeast Asia by 1972. The majority of U.S. Marines "in country" were fire support or communications specialists and the advisors with the South Vietnamese Marine Corps. The TQLC, or VNMC in English, was formed from former French commando units after the 1954 cease fire that established North and South Vietnam. An elite unit by any standards and closely associated with the U.S. Marine Corps, the VNMC had been fighting the Communists for over a decade. Those American Marines selected to serve with the VNMC were considered the "chosen few" for being the last Marines in combat and for the exotic nature of their assignment. As advisors, they wore the distinctive Green Beret and "tiger stripe" battle dress of the VNMC. As part of the South Vietnamese national reserve, two Marine brigades were deployed along the demilitarized zone with the 3rd ARVN Division following the departure of American combat units from Military Region 1 in 1971. For them the war was not over yet and a major test of their efforts came during the Communist Spring Invasion that started on 30 March 1972.

Easter Sunday, 2 April, proved to be a fateful day for the 3rd ARVN Division defending northern Quang Tri Province. After three days of continuous artillery fire and tank-infantry assaults, it appeared that the North Vietnamese were making their main attack along the axis of the national highway, QL-1. At this time Camp Carroll and Mai Loc fire support bases to the west were still in friendly hands, but all resistance to the north of the Cam Lo River had crumbled. The 308th NVA Division's thrust from the DMZ to the south had gained momentum as each ARVN outpost and fire support base fell. Intelligence reports estimated that three NVA mechanized divisions were attacking with approximately 10,000 infantry, 150 T-54 and PT-76 tanks, 75 tracked anti-aircraft vehicles, one artillery regiment of 47 130mm guns, and anti-aircraft missile units.

By mid-day Easter Sunday, nothing was on the QL-1 axis between the enemy and the coveted Quang Tri City except a river, a bridge and a battalion of Vietnamese Marines and tanks. With them on the ground in MR-1 were the advisors. The 3rd VNMC Battalion, with Captain John W. Ripley as its sole American advisor, was spread along Route 9 from Cam Lo to Dong Ha. Ripley was on his second tour in Vietnam, a U.S. Naval Academy graduate with experience from Force Recon and Royal Marine exchange tours. He provided "advise" and fire support coordination to the 700 man unit on the south side of the river sent to gain enough time for the 3rd ARVN Division to organize a new defense line south of the Thach Han River.

With the report of approaching tanks, Major Le Ba Binh, the 3rd VNMC battalion commander, was ordered by his brigade commander to hold Dong Ha. The brigade commander sent four jeep-mounted 106mm recoilless rifles north for support. Also sent forward were 42 brand-new M48 main battle tanks of the 20th ARVN Tank Battalion. Binh was ordered to "hold Dong Ha at all costs." Ripley was told to expect the worst: a column of Communist PT-76 and T-54 tanks were approaching, refugees were clogging the roads out of Dong Ha, and no further units were available to help. A large red North Vietnamese flag was seen flying over the railroad bridge, NVA infantrymen were storming across both spans as the Marines, and tanks arrived. Ripley recalled an "absolute fire storm" of Communist artillery fire hitting Dong Ha at this point. Enemy tanks appeared on the horizon sending up rooster tails of dust as they barreled down QL-1. Naval gunfire from American destroyers in the Tonkin Gulf had some effect on the enemy advance as oily black columns of smoke rose over the north bank of the river. But this was not enough to stop them. At 1200, the ARVN M48s began firing at the NVA tank column, knocking out six Communist vehicles.

At about 1215, as the first NVA tank nosed out onto the north side of the highway bridge, Vietnamese Marine Sergeant Huynh Van Luom, a veteran of many years fighting, took two M72 light anti-tank assault weapons (LAAW) and walked up to the south side of the bridge. Although he was a section leader, he moved forward alone. As he reached the bridge, he took two ammunition boxes filled with dirt and a single roll of concertina wire and placed them in front of him. It was a ludicrous situation; the 90-pound Marine crouched in the firing position to battle a 40-ton behemoth bearing down on his meager fortification. Luom coolly extended both LAAWs as the NVA tank started across the bridge.

The tank jerked to a halt, perhaps the tank commander could not believe his eyes; he stopped dead in his tracks as he watched the lone Marine take aim. Luom fired; the round went high and to the right. The tank started to ease forward. Luom picked up the second rocket, aimed and fired. The round ricocheted off the bow, detonating on the turret-ring, jamming the turret. The enemy tank commander backed off the bridge, making the worst possible decision he could have. All at once, the Marines along the river saw that enemy armor could be stopped.

The whole incident took only a few seconds. Sergeant Luom grinned and the whole front breathed easier. Captain Ripley gave Sergeant Luom credit for "single-handedly stopping the momentum of the entire enemy attack." At 1245, the ARVN division command post radioed Major James

Picture of the diorama at the U.S. Naval Academy depicting Capt. John W. Ripley hanging under the Dong Ha Bridge over the Cua Viet River, as he placed the explosives provided by Major James E. Smock, U.S. Army Advisor. This was accomplished under fire, in full view of the North Vietnamese riflemen and tanks poised to attack across the bridge. The enemy's firing came to a stop when the bridge blew; they would not cross at Dong Ha.

E. Smock, U.S. Army advisor with the 20th ARVN Tank Battalion, authorization to blow the Dong Ha Bridge immediately. If necessary, additional demolitions would be sent up and that higher headquarters had been informed of the decision. When Ripley heard this, he replied, "He had always wanted to blow a bridge." Although he was modest, almost shy, no man could have been better qualified to do the job, with demolition expertise from U.S. Army Ranger School and the Royal Marine's special boat squadron. As Ripley walked forward toward the bridge, Major Smock on an ARVN tank called, "Hey Marine, climb aboard and let's go blow a bridge." The two Americans with two M48 tanks moved forward to within 100 meters of the bridge. Still in defilade, the tanks stopped at this point. Ripley and Smock dismounted, shielded from enemy view by an old bunker. From the bunker to the bridge was open space swept by enemy artillery and small arms fire. The sun was bright, the weather had cleared, but there were no aircraft overhead or naval gunfire coming in to provide covering fire. The Marines in forward positions fired at the north bank as the two advisors came forward.

The two men ran across the open space. They found ARVN engineers, stacking 500 pounds of TNT and C-4 plastic explosive at the juncture of the bridge and the approach ramp. The ARVN engineers, however, had placed the explosives in such a position that upon detonation, the bridge would merely "flap" in place and not have dropped. Ripley, quickly surveying the situation, realized that the explosives would have to be placed along the girders under the bridge. A high chain-linked fence topped by barbed wire prevented access to the underpinnings of the bridge. After a quick conference with Smock, it was agreed that once Ripley cleared the fence, Smock would lift the TNT over the fence and Ripley, in turn, would place it underneath this spans.

Swinging his body up and over the fence, Ripley barely cleared the concertina, shredding his uniform. Clearing this obstacle, and with a satchel charge and some blasting caps, the Marine started hand-over-hand above the water along the first girder. About halfway out over the swiftly flowing water, he tried to swing himself up into the steal girders by hooking his heels on either side of the beam. It was then that he realized that he still had on his webbing and had his rifle slung over his shoulder. All at once, the weight was oppressive. As he was hanging by his hands with

Captain John Ripley (left), Advisor to the 3d Vietnamese Marine Battalion and Major Le Ba Binh – next right – battalion commander, take a break during the battle for Dong Ha, April 1972 – four days after the destruction of the Dong Ha Bridge which halted attacking NVA. Photo by David Burnett, courtesy of Col. John Ripley, USMC.

explosives, web gear, weapon, watched by the NVA soldiers, Ripley made another effort to secure a foothold on the beam. His arms ached with pain, his finger grasp felt insecure, and he could not hang there indefinitely. After several attempts to swing his body, he lodged his heels on the beam. Working his way up into the steal of the bridge, he discovered that the support girders were separated by practically the width of the ammunition crates in which the explosives had been packed.

Crawling back and forth between the beams, Ripley placed the demolitions in a staggered alignment between the six girders. Major Smock, remaining at the fence, muscled the 50-pound boxes near the five channels created by the six beams by climbing the fence each time and placing them within Ripley's reach. As each channel was mined, it was necessary for Ripley to drop down from one beam and swing over the next, very similar to a high wire act in a circus.

As the Marine laboriously dragged each crate of TNT down the chute formed by the legs of each of the beams, Major Smock became impatient with Ripley's meticulous manner and concerned about the small-arms fire from the north bank, 50 meters away. He called, "Hey, you dumb jarhead, that isn't necessary… What are you doing that for?" "You tankers don't know anything," Ripley assured Smock. The charges had to be placed diagonally in order to torque the span from its abutment. Smock insisted that there was enough power to blow that bridge and "three more like it." Nevertheless, despite the inter-service rivalry, the bridge had to be destroyed on the first try. There would be no time for a second attempt.

After lifting all the boxes of explosives to Ripley, Smock sat down and lit a cigarette while Ripley relaxed amidst the steel girders. Finally, the explosives in place, Ripley took the electric blasting caps from his pocket and crimped them to the communications wire being used to detonate the charge. Clearing the fence, he ran the wire to the burning wreckage of a nearby "Jeep." As a precaution, he had cut 30 minutes of time fuse before attempting an electrical detonation using the vehicle's battery. Ripley touched the wire to either terminal, but the bridge did not blow. Now it seemed the fate of South Vietnam's northern provinces rested on a burning fuse sputtering its way toward 500-pounds of high explosive.

After what seemed an eternity, the time fuse neared its end. The telltale smoke trail was now out of view. Smock and Ripley "waited and hoped." Suddenly, the bridge blew! The span, curling in the predicted twisting manner, was severed from the berm "and settled into the river." The smoking open space between the north and south banks was a beautiful sight for the two Americans. At 1630, Ripley reported to division headquarters that the bridge had been destroyed, and that Major Smock had demolished the railroad bridge upstream.

Air strikes by South Vietnamese A-1 Skyraiders hit the armored column backed up north of the bridge. All firing stopped, there was a calm for a few moments, then, on the north side, noise was evident once more as NVA tanks shifted their positions to make room for PT-76 amphibious tanks to come forward to the river's edge. The enemy was determined to cross. Ripley saw four of them ready to cross and immediately called a naval gunfire mission. The gunfire support ship sailed within the five-fathom curve and let go with a salvo. All four tanks were destroyed on the riverbank; Ripley recalling that this destroyer probably was one of the few ships in the Navy that rated four enemy tanks painted on her stacks. Subsequently, a B-52 bombing strike, which had been scheduled for that area, silenced the remaining tank activity to the north and east of Dong Ha, for the time being.

With their armored thrusts thwarted at the Dong Ha and Cua Viet areas, the determined Communists exerted pressure elsewhere. The Cam Lo Bridge to the west was the only available crossing point and the NVA effort shifted in that direction. More naval gunfire was called for and the fire from the guns of the destroyers again squelched enemy movement as all night long, hundreds of naval projectiles were called in upon the enemy. The battle for Dong Ha was still in doubt, but there was no question the Communist armored-assault had been halted by the efforts of "a few good men" on Easter Sunday. For their actions that day, Captain Ripley was awarded the Navy Cross-America's second highest award for valor-and Major Smock, the Silver Star Medal-the third highest award for valor. But John Ripley recalled VNMC Sergeant Luom's action in stopping the first tank at the bridge as the "...bravest single act of heroism I've ever heard of, witnessed or experienced."

"For he who fights with me this day will be my brother."
—*Henry V, Act 4, Scene III*

Dong Ha Bridge burning 4 days after destruction, 6 April 1972. At the far right are enemy armored vehicles exposed to air attacks and unable to advance.

THE INCURSION INTO CAMBODIA, 1970

Colonel Hoang Tich Thong

Security and Politics

During Tet Mau Than, 1968, a number of cities and towns in South Vietnam were attacked by the NVA and the so-called "National Front for the Liberation of the South". In doing so, the Communists violated the three days of cease-fire that was organized by both sides for the new year. They managed to temporarily invade a few areas, not before inflicting heavy losses to civilian lives and properties. The historical city of Hue suffered the most damage. After the ARVN successfully quashed the insurgent, the situation was calm for a number of years. As the Tet Offensive had taken a heavy toll on the enemy, the political situation became less tense, and both sides agreed to attend the Paris Peace Talks.

After the crushing defeat of the NVA in the Tet Offensive, Ho Chi Minh deteriorated, and died frustrated and disappointed in September 1969. The remaining leaders bent to American pressure and attended the peace talks.

The Enemy

After being routed in the Tet Offensive of 1968, and in the 2nd Wave of attack in May of the same year, the NVA and the National Front for the Liberation of the South could not afford to launch another full–scale offensive. Their activities were reduced to small skirmishes, while their big units retreated across the boarder to Cambodia to restructure and retrain. Their regional infrastructure was weakened as units were caught and annihilated every time they emerged. Later, Intelligence reported that VC regional commanders from the company level upwards had been replaced by commanders from the north. The regional forces became more and more dependent on the North for political and military support.

The Republic of VietNam

Although the ARVN had successfully counterattacked in the Tet Offensive, and in the Second Wave of Attack in May, South Vietnam also suffered losses. Many civilians and troops were lost, and properties were damaged. Hue suffered the most. The NVA had captured thousands of civilians, troops and government officials during their short occupation of South Vietnamese regions. To hasten their retreat, they massacred all their prisoners. That crime has remained an unforgivable and unforgettable act in the minds of the South Vietnamese, even to today. Though the ARVN held the enemy in contempt, they were surprised at how low the NVA were for breaking the cease-fire organized for the New Year.

After the Tet Offensive, the situation in all four tactical zones became calmer, and security was high. The spirits in the hamlets, and the villages under government control, soared. Confidence returned to the regional and popular forces, but the calm was temporary. The enemy were not completely paralyzed.

Weapons, manpower, and supplies were still coming south along the Ho Chi Minh Trail from the North. The favorite route was via the port in Sihanoukville, Cambodia, into III and IV Corps of South Vietnam. The enemy benefited from the Cambodian Government's hostility towards South Vietnam, and so were able to freely use Cambodian ports. Their recovery was marked by the sorties they carried across the border into South Vietnam. To stop the sorties, and to crush the enemy completely, the ARVN planned an operation to smash the NVA sanctuaries in Cambodia.

Incursion into Cambodia

Early in 1970, the political situation in Cambodia changed. General Lon Nol, the Premier of Cambodia, led a coup that overthrew Prince Sihanouk. Sihanouk had been visiting Beijing and North Vietnam at the time. The new government's policy was friendly to western powers, and opposed Communism. This was very favorable to South Vietnam. During the transitional period, the Cambodian Government was too busy consolidating power to battle two enemies (the Khmer Rouge and the NVA) at once. The NVA practically had full-rein along the border from Sihanoukville to the Laotian border to the north. Hence, General Lon Nol agreed to allow the ARVN to perform incursions across the border. The goals were:

a)   To annihilate the NVA which were occupying Cambodia;

b)   To help Cambodian troops in organizing and training (with help from the US), so that they could become self-proficient in defense in the future.

The ARVN performed the incursions without the support of the US, and without the participation of American advisors. The incursion was composed of two prongs: one from III Corps, and the other from IV Corps. There were also units from the rest of the Army Corps.

The III Corps prong was commanded by Lieutenant General Do Cao Tri. The IV Corps prong was led by Lieutenant General Ngo Du. The Airborne Division was to participate with III Corps, while the Marines were to fight with IV Corps.

Marine Activities

I. Marine Brigade B.

Marine Brigade B, commanded by Colonel Ton That Soan, had three Marine Battalions, and an Amphibious Task Force led by Navy Colonel Thong. It started from the line of departure at Chau Doc, and sailed upstream along the Mekong. On reaching the border, the battalion landed on the right river bank. The Marines advanced to Neak Luong, while the Amphibious Task Force patrolled along the river to support the operation. The landing and preparation for the operation were uneventful. There were no confrontations. The Marine Artillery was air-lifted from Chau Doc to the area of Operation.

The countryside was barren with villages scattered here and there. The advancement was not at all difficult. The enemy had probably foreseen our plans, and had moved deeper into the Cambodian territories in the north. Only small units were left behind to delay the Marines. In a period of three days, the Marines killed numerous NVA, and destroyed a remarkable number of warehouses containing rice, medicine, and weapons. Marine Brigade B then deployed around Neak Luong, co-operating with Cambodian forces in charge of the security of the region.

The local government then requested another operation. The 3rd Marine Battalion commanded by Lieutenant Colonel Nguyen Nang Bao, was airlifted to the left side of the Mekong, to an area situated about 50-60 km southwest of the capital, Phnom Penh.

The operation only lasted a day, and was a pointless exercise as the enemy had withdrawn the previous day. Regarding the distribution of Communists, the NVA controlled the east, while the Khmer Rouge mastered the west of Cambodia. Marine Brigade B continued to expand the safety perimeter of the city, helping Cambodian units to evolve and defend. Marine Brigade A later took over, and Brigade B returned to base camp.

II. Marine Brigade A.

By the time Marine Brigade B was in Cambodia, Marine Brigade A, commanded by Colonel Hoang Tich Thong, was already performing operations in Chuong Thien Province. IV Corps Headquarters ordered military trucks to transport Brigade A to Chau Doc, where the Navy took them to Neak Luong Ferry. Marine Brigade A carried on with the tasks of Brigade B. On the agenda was the liberation of Prey Veng Province, which was under NVA occupation. The province was 10 km northeast of Neak Luong. The Cambodian troops had been defending inside a camp situated south of Prey Veng City.

Before planning the operation, I made an observation trip by helicopter to the would-be battlefield. From above, the city of Prey Veng was very beautiful. Neat and tidy houses opened on to wide, tree-lined avenues. It was only after the battle that I had the chance to appreciate the architecture fully. The buildings and streets were very much influenced by the French.

The population was very thin, as the majority had fled. A few houses were already marred by 122mm NVA rockets. The terrain was not overly vegetated, and was quite suitable for helicopter landings. The drawback was that the enemy could hide within houses near the edge of the city and fire at us during the landing.

Progress of the Operation

Two Marine Battalions were to be airlifted by helicopters to a landing zone west of the city. Another battalion was to stay at Neak Luong as a reserve. ARVN helicopters were to be in charge of the airlift of troops. The helicopters were to receive fire support from gunships and the Artillery in case of strong enemy reactions. The aim was to minimize damage to the city.

At the scheduled time, a Marine Company was safely airlifted near the city. They were able to take up positions under the rows of trees that lined the avenues. The Cambodian officer accompanying me contacted a Cambodian unit south of the city, which reported that the NVA had already occupied large areas to the north of the City. I gave the go-ahead for the rest of the airlift, which was completed at noon. Two companies advanced simultaneously from the northeast. Nothing happened until the two prongs approached the northern regions of the city, and were confronted by the enemy. The NVA troops hid in two-story buildings, and shot down at the approaching Marines. To avoid the bullets, the Marines skirted along the side of the houses. The fighting continued well into the night. When it was far too dark, we stopped advancing. But the fighting immediately broke out again at the break of day. The enemy were making a very firm stand. I ordered the two battalions to annihilate them at all costs with the help of gunships and the Artillery. At noon, the enemy were dislodged from the houses at the north ends of the streets. The Marines continued to evict them, house by house. Many NVA soldiers were captured or killed, and all abandoned weapons were seized. As evening approached, the NVA fled, running northwards out of the city.

After two days of fighting, Marine Brigade A succeeded in liberating the city, and sustained minimal losses. To help the regional government recover authority, and to enable the Cambodians to protect themselves, two battalions of Marine Brigade A were maintained in the area for quite some time. During that time, Search and Destroy operations were organized. I was told by IV Corps to fly to the position of Colonel Khoi's 3rd Armor Brigade to receive a squadron of APC's But at the last minute, the order was cancelled, and Brigade A had to carry out tasks with its own facilities and equipment.

After a couple of days of rest, the Brigade A deployed 10 km northwards, but there was no remarkable fighting as the NVA had already retreated further north. A few rice warehouse were detected though.

Once Prey Veng was safe, the Marine Brigade A marched back to Neak Luong. Along the way, the Marines helped the Cambodian regional forces rebuild their camps and bunkers.

The communist prisoners of war were around 19-20 years of age. They were scrawny, jaundiced, malnourished creatures who were obviously unhealthy. Most of them suffered from malaria. On interrogation, they said that they had just arrived from the north along the Ho Chi Minh Trail. We gave them food and cigarettes, which sent them into ecstasy. They admitted that they had not expected to be so well treated—their commanders had petrified them with tales of our inhumane treatment of POWs. Many were students, who had been dragged out of school and mobilized.

Back in Neak Luong, Marine Brigade A continued to carry out raids on suspected enemy positions, and closely cooperated with the newly formed Cambodian Brigade commanded by Colonel Pre-meas. He spoke fluent French and Vietnamese. He was schooled in France to become a Quartermaster. He was a close friend of Colonel Lon Nol's younger brother. After the Marines returned to Vietnam, he was promoted to Brigadier General. No one knows whether he survived the Khmer Rouge. Colonel Lon Nol's younger brother was executed along with the Premier.

To the newly formed Cambodian Brigade, the Marines gave all the weapons seized from the NVA. The Cambodians generally used weapons from communist countries—most of the weapons came from China. The relationship between the Cambodians and Vietnamese was very cooperative and amicable. There were minor skirmished between the troops, but these were easily resolved by the Military Police. The Cambodian citizens and troops in general were very supportive of the Marines.

A week after, the Marine Brigade A was ordered to perform an operation northwest of Phnom Penh. As before, one battalion remained in Neak Luong, whilst the other two participated. Ferries transported the troops over the river, to the military trucks that were to take them along Route 1 to Phnom Penh. The Cambodian people came out and cheered us warmly. The convoy stopped 30km out of Phnom Penh, on the road leading to Kompong Cham. The Marine Brigade A stationed south of the road in preparation for the next day's operation.

The following day, the Brigade was transported across the Bassac River. The Brigade Headquarters and Marine Artillery remained at the camp to support the operation. After the fall of Sihanouk, security in the area near the Bassac River was very unstable. The NVA had retreated here, after their unfortunate rendezvous with the Marines. The terrain was bushy, and there were many quaint villages and splendid pagodas. One particularly magnificent pagoda was visited annually by Prince Sihanouk.

During the first day, the Marines were unchallenged. The following day, one battalion confronted the enemy, but the ensuing fighting was minimal. The Marines soon drove them back. The NVA were forced to seek refuge in the largest of the pagodas. The Marines were unable to turn their guns at the sacred pagoda, so camped outside instead. That night, the NVA managed to sneak away. The following day, the Marines continued their Search and Destroy Operations, but the enemy had completely disappeared. So, the operation ended, unremarkably, and Brigade A moved back to Neak Luong.

A few days later, IV Corps Headquarters issued the news that President Nguyen Van Thieu, the South Vietnamese Head of State, was going to visit the Cambodian Head of States—Cheng Heng and Premier Lon Nol. The meeting was to take place at the base camp of Marine Brigade A at Neak Luong. IV Corps was in charge of organizing the meeting. The Marine Brigade appointed a unit to carry out the military salute, while the other two were told to take care of security and the presidential motorcade. Troops were stationed all along Route 1, that ran from Neak Luong to Xoai Rieng Province.

In the days that followed the presidential visit, Marine Brigade A performed operations with "44" Special District Units commanded by Colonel Hanh to liberate Route 5 from Phnom Penh to Sihanoukville, Intelligence sources had reported that there were still some enemy elements in areas around the Piknil Pass. The enemy were interfering with communications. Cambodian regional forces were unable to protect the route. Within a very short time, Pik Nil Pass fell under the control of the ARVN. The enemy did not resist—most had retreated to the North. The route was reopened, allowing for normal circulation. The Marines then handed the position back to the Cambodians to man.

Thus, the Marines completed a successful incursion into Cambodia. The NVA, who had used Eastern Cambodia as a springboard to launch attacks on South Vietnam, had to retreat north to the Cambodian-Laotian border. The Cambodian Brigade, newly formed and inexperienced, were at least set in key positions. Though the Vietnamese withdrew, South Vietnam and the US still supported General Lon Nol's stand against the ever-increasing Khmer Rouge, which was backed by China.

The incursion gained security for III and IV Corps. The enemy no longer launched large scale attacks in the ARVN. Only unremarkable skirmishes persisted. The peace lasted till 1972, when the NVA launched a massive attack on Quang Tri Province in I Corps. Binh Long Province in III Corps was also attacked in the Summer of 1972.

Que Son, South Vietnam, September 1970; Senior Marine Advisor, Colonel Francis Tief and G–3 Advisor Major Rivers, consider tactical plans of the 258th Brigade. After the conclusion of the Cambodian incursion, the brigade was sent North. In early March 1971, brigades 147 and 258 moved into Laos as part of Operation Lam Son 719.

MARINE TRAINING

The Vietnamese Marine Training Command had the overall responsibility for the training requirements, program development and implementation and out-of-country school attendance and training for the Marine Corps. In July of 1964, the Recruit Training Center was established at Thu Duc (a small town located about 12 mi. north of Saigon), and by the end of the year had graduated 1,464 recruits. These recruits, for the most part, were trained by Vietnamese noncommissioned officers who had completed the drill instructor course at the U.S. Marine Corps Recruit Depot in San Diego—which served to instill much of the institutional aspects, discipline and traditions of the U.S.M.C through them to the Vietnamese Marine. Also, in the coming years, many of the Vietnamese small unit leaders would attend OJT (on-the-job training) with U.S. Marines in Okinawa. Vietnamese officers would attend schools and more formal training in the United States when possible. Most battalion commanders were graduates of the amphibious warfare school.

The U.S. advisors had a great amount of influence within the VNMC Training Command due to their knowledge and expertise in training doctrine. Battlefield skills, physical conditioning, discipline, small unit leadership and motivation was stressed. They had attended the "MATA" course (Military Assistance Training Advisory) at Fort Bragg, North Carolina. It was a six-week course during which half of their time was spent learning the Vietnamese language. The rest of the time was devoted to studying and understanding Vietnamese customs, tradition, history, ethnic problems and counter-insurgency.

The training, professionalism and "*spirit dé corps,*" produced a 14,000-man fighting force with approximately 55 U.S. Marine Advisors by the end of the war.

Vietnamese Marines received the same tough training that every US Marine faced, knowing they would see combat. As part of all marine challenges, here, they conduct "Wet Net" training, 1971.

VNMC Master Sergeant Theem, USMC-trained, and wearing the traditional campaign hat of the Marine drill instuctor, corrects a Vietnamese Marine recruit.

Vietnamese Marine Training at VNMC "Boot Camp," Thu Duc, 1969.

A Vietnamese Drill Instructor gives one-to-one tips to a recruit on a demanding tactical course.

Lieutenant General Herman Nickerson, Commanding General, III Marine Amphibious Force and Colonel Lance V. Corbett, Senior Advisor, Vietnamese Marine Corps, 1969.

Advisor, Captain Tom Taylor, on radio – standing – with Mobile Riverine Force in the Mekong Delta.

Captain Joseph P. Hoar, assistant Task Force Advisor, stands by his field radio aboard a U.S. Navy Utility Landing Craft (LCU) during a troop movement to the operating area. The Danang-based LCUs transported two VNMC battalions of Task Force Alfa from Dong Ha to a point near the coastline. The movement was a part of a search and destroy operation near the Demilitarized Zone (DMZ), 21 December 1966. Hoar went on to become a 4 Star General and retired as the Commander of the Southern Command.

Lieutenant Bruce Mellon, Advisor to the South Vietnamese Marine Brigade G-1, June '66 to June '67.

VNMC Advisor wearing the camouflage uniform, "sea-wave" or "tiger-stripes," with the VNMC Signal Battalion insignia on his right sleeve.

Advisor Capt. Cyril L. Kammeier, USMC with Asst. Battalion Commander, 3d Battalion, VNMC prepare to embark aboard LCM's for transit from Can Tho to Cam Mau via inland waterways in April 1969. Radio operator and enlisted aide are at right. A strobe light, on the right shoulder harness; flashlight, on left shoulder; .45 pistol; first aid kit; survival knife; flack jacket; maps; helmet and VNMC uniform were the "in vogue" uniform of the day for field advisors. In garrison, a green beret with VNMC insignia was worn in lieu of the helmet. 1968.

Major Raymond L. Gaboury (left) and Captain Joseph P. Hoar, Marine Advisors, in the field, 1967. On the right side of the photograph a Vietnamese Marine has a bottle protruding from his pack, undoubtedly filled with **nuoc mam** or **nuoc cham**, a fermented fish sauce that accompanies all meals in Vietnam.

Going away party for Marine Advisor Arch L. Early, June 1966.

Captain William J.P. Mannix, USMC, Advisor to the Amphibious Support Battalion of the Vietnamese Marine Corps, adjusts the frequency on the radio prior to beginning of boat drill. His headgear is the utility cover in olive green – the Marines called it "sage green." The Vietnamese Marine Sergeant to his right, wears a full size rank insignia on the front of his shirt instead of on the shoulder straps. He is wearing a mixture of American web gear.

MARINE GORDON W. KEISER

Col. Gordon W. Keiser, USMC (Ret)

My first tour in Vietnam was in 1967, as advisor to the 21st Ranger Battalion in I Corps. That experience turned out to be especially useful for my second tour, which was as battalion and brigade advisor to the Vietnamese Marines, 1972-1973.

By the time I got back to the field in mid-summer 1972, the situation was that of conventional rather than guerrilla warfare; i.e., it was more or less linear, with the NVA on one side and us on the other. There was little or no danger, such as mines, booby traps and snipers, behind our lines. The Vietnamese Marines were dug-in in the vicinity of Quang Tri, facing NVA units similarly dug-in. Both sides had artillery and other supporting forces.

One of the most memorable aspects of my service with the Vietnamese Marines was the NVA use of artillery. In 1967, I noted that the Vietnamese, enemy and friendly, were excellent mortarmen and communicators. Soon after arriving in 1972, I discovered that they were even better gunners. Unfortunately, the South Vietnamese were outgunned in terms of the number of pieces and in range. NVA artillery—especially 130mm and 122mm guns—was quite effective. It was rapid; it was accurate; it was terrifying. After enduring sporadic shelling for a few months and one major barrage of only a few hours duration, I developed great sympathy for the WWI and II troops who faced such fire for months on end.

Our chief advantage in supporting arms was air power, despite the high altitudes from which U.S. aircraft were required to deliver ordnance as the war wound down. One day, another Marine advisor and I were directing air strikes on targets around the Quang Tri Citadel. Following several missions, the USAF forward air controller (airborne) told us he was going to try some "smart" ordnance, which was a brand-new concept at the time. After numerous drops, no bomb hit nearer than half a mile from its target. We asked the FAC(A) as to cost of the many bombs expended, which came to roughly $300,000, and advised him to go back to smart pilots and dumb bombs.

It is a source of considerable irritation to me that large segments of our society—including some veterans—believe the South Vietnamese Armed Forces were uniformly incompetent and even cowardly. Like the accepted Hollywood view that U.S. units were uniformly riddled with indiscipline and fraggings, nothing could be farther from the truth. So, I would like to take this opportunity to express my appreciation of and fondness for the many superb South Vietnamese Army and Marine troops with whom I served. I was proud of them and honored to be at their side.

Captain Scott Bentley and First Lieutenant Richard Bruce, directing fire support for the Vietnamese Marines.

I'LL BE OKAY

Marine Thomas E. Campbell

Big John Hopkins was powerful and impressive—in both appearance and personality. Standing six-foot four with a barrel chest over a slim waist, he was a natural jock, born for the football field. He fulfilled that destiny at the U.S. Naval Academy where, as an All-American tackle, he captained the 1955 Navy team that defeated Ole Miss in the Sugar Bowl. He had a huge head, dark hair and eyebrows, and dark eyes over a classic Roman nose, and was one of the handsomest men I have ever known. When he stood or walked, it was with an easy, natural slouch that seemed at first to be apologizing for his size. But in fact, that was a tool. He was bigger than most men, so he had to stoop down to look them in the eye while he explained—always impatiently—how things obviously were at present, and how he fully expected them to be. There always seemed to be a large gap between these two extremes. Whenever he spoke, his hands and arms were in continual motion. He had been raised in Brooklyn, New York, and had an accent and an attitude that could have come from nowhere else. The expression "in-your-face" could have been coined about him. His ability to convey with urgency and power his duly considered opinions on everything—from beer, to boats, to small-unit tactics, to the U.S. position in the turbulent 20th-century world—made him the center of any unit, group, liberty run, or bull session he joined. Few had neutral feelings about Big John, and over the years, he won many devoted friends and accumulated some bitter enemies.

In 1965, Big John became the senior advisor to the 2nd Battalion—The Crazy Water Buffaloes—of the South Vietnamese Marines. I was his assistant. Well into our one-year tour, we were operating in Binh Dinh Province, where it was said that any Vietnamese who was not a Viet Cong himself had relatives who were. The Viet Cong and North Vietnamese Army units considered Binh Dinh their own personal turf, and there were firefights every day and probes, large and small, every night. We were made to feel unwelcome there, and after we failed to show the good grace to leave, the pressure mounted daily.

After three nights of heavy attacks against our positions, we decided to strike back with a spoiling attack, to throw them off their timing. Supported by air strikes, artillery, and naval gunfire, we advanced toward their staging areas with two Marine battalions abreast. After overrunning several other positions, we found ourselves face-to-face with a North Vietnamese Army Regiment—a terrible thing to behold. They drew us in close to minimize the effectiveness of our supporting arms—grabbing us by the belt, so to speak—then lit off one of their classic L-shaped ambushes. Fortunately, neither of our battalions was in the main killing zone, but the shear volume of devastating fire told us that we had walked into a trap of still-unknown but ominous dimensions. The task force commander ordered a withdrawal, but anyone who ever has tried to break contact with Communist Vietnamese units knows what happened next: they just held onto our belt and moved along with us, staying too close for us to use indirect fires against them.

Big John called me on the radio. "Your buddy (Vietnamese counterpart) will be ordered by my buddy to withdraw back through our positions."

"We're still in heavy contact here," I replied. "We've got five killed and eight wounded. It will take at least an hour."

"Roger. Move as fast as you can."

Two hours later, we straggled to the rear through a treeline, carrying a dozen dead and 30 wounded. Big John was sitting by a tree with a radio on his back.

"Where is your radioman?" I asked.

"I sent him back with the command group."

"So what are you doing here by yourself?"

"I'm advisin'. Tommy my boy," he said with that great smile of his. "Go find my buddy. You're his advisor until I get back."

"You better watch out, Big John…."

"Don't worry about me, I'll be OK," he said. Then he began to crawl toward the enemy, talking in his cocky Brooklynese to the airborne forward air controller overhead, who had four A-4 Sky Hawk aircraft on station.

As I move toward the rear, looking for the 2nd Battalion's commander, there seemed to be a lull in the incoming fire—until a barrage of mortar rounds began crunching into our units. I dove for cover and looked up. I will never forget the sight: a Navy A-4 was coming in low, heading straight for me. He was so low that I could see the pilot's face and feel the heat from his tail pipe, as he pulled up with napalm tanks tumbling from his wings. To my horror, it looked as though the strike had gone in right where I last had seen Big John.

I started to yell into my radio handset. No response came from John, but the air controller answered it; he had lost contact with John, too. The A-4s were turning the target area into an inferno. I sat down behind a big tree, with my back to the scene, still trying to raise Big John on the radio. It suddenly dawned on me that the mortar barrage—and even the small arms fire—had stopped. I tried the radio again, in deep despair:

US Marine Advisor is conspicuous among smaller Vietnamese.

"Leatherneck Two—Two Alpha. How do you read? Over."

"I read you just fine, Tommy," said Big John, walking up and sitting down beside me. "Hey! How about a cigarette for a real combat veteran? I ruined this whole day for those guys over there, and I deserve one." Big John smoked a lot, but never bought any. It was a matter of principle.

Then I saw why he had not answered my calls. His handset was shot in two, and two bullets lodged in the radio set had saved him from being hit in the back.

Handing him a cigarette, I said, "Big John, the Marine Corps is going to make you pay for the radio. You signed for it."

"Tommy, don't you worry about me. This is clearly a combat loss. I'll be OK." After our advisor tour, we saw each other as often as we could but never served in the same outfit again. I met his family that he was so proud of, and we stayed in touch. I was serving in Hawaii in the early 1970's when I read the headline about an altercation at an Oceanside, California, bar that had involved three battalion commanders from the 1st Marine Division. Big John was one of them. I called him.

"Big John, it's not good. There are people out there who either take a very dim view of the whole thing, or are your enemies, or both."

"You're right, Tommy, but there's about a dozen dim-viewers and two dozen enemies. If the numbers were switched, there'd be no sweat. Remember, Tommy, friends come and go; enemies accumulate. But my friends still outnumber my enemies, and the ones who love me love me more than my enemies hate me. So I'm ahead of the game."

It hurt for a while, but in time, the Oceanside hassle wore off and Big John continued up the promotion ladder—the hard way, after getting passed over for colonel once and brigadier general twice. By then, he had developed a distinct limp, and I questioned him about it.

"Oh, my leg still acts up. They say my heart is fine, but my blood pressure keeps going up and down. My arteries are no good. I might have diabetes. But who cares? We have places to go and things to do and see."

But by then, he was alone.

He and his wife Dorothy had split up, and then she had died. There was a sadness to him; a bitterness too. But after he got promoted to brigadier general, Big John's life seemed to turn around. Then he made his second star, and the sadness, bitterness, and limp were gone. He had things to do and Marines to take care of. He was looking good and was at the top of his game.

Big John was a tactician, not an office pinky or headquarters Pogue. And he got to make his final war-fighting run in the Persian Gulf War. Soon after the Iraqi invasion of Kuwait, he took the 7th Marine Expeditionary Brigade—the closest thing to an armored brigade that the Marines had ever fielded—into Saudi Arabia, marrying up with weapons and equipment brought in by ships of the Maritime Prepositioning Force, confirming the strategic and tactical validity of a Vet-untested deployment concept, then ten years old. Relieving the lightly equipped trip-wire force of the 82nd Airborne Division, which would have been little more than a speed bump in the way of Saddam Hussein's armored columns if they had chosen to drive into Saudi Arabia, Big John put on his game face and stirred up enough dust to deter further Iraqi thrusts until the U.S. Army and all its heavy gear arrived some weeks later. He had saved our bacon with his fighting spirit and tactical expertise.

After that short war, Big John retired as a major general and went back to Fallbrook, California, beyond the back gate of Camp Pendleton. After we talked about my patterning a character in my upcoming novel about him, I asked how he was feeling.

"Well you know you always told me I had to clean up my act. So sometimes I act like I'm not listening, but I always listen. This diabetes was getting out of hand, so I just had to change some things. And I did. So, don't worry about me. I'll be OK."

When I got home one night last April, the voice of another former advisor, Mack Dube, was on my answering machine, deep and full of emotion. I knew what Mack was going to say before he said it. Big John Hopkins was not okay anymore. He was dead.

On 19 April 1998, the Marine Corps buried one of its greatest spirits and interpreters of what the Corps really is. Big John personified the notion that the Marine Corps is much more an idea than just another military organization. The Corps is, in fact, whatever we Marines make of it. It is said that spirit is more important than knowledge. Big John had plenty of knowledge—and his spirit always came shining through.

His spirit always was present in his voice when he talked, and that is how I will choose to remember him: young, strong, and unbeatable, with a radio on his back, telling me, "Don't worry about me. I'll be OK," as he crawled forward to take on a North Vietnamese regiment by himself. I surely hope he is okay now. He deserves some rest.

I always have regarded my Dad and Big John as my personal heroes. I never told either one of them that while they lived. I wish I had.

But I think they know!

Advisors adjust fire (artillery) on enemy occupied village.

MARINE ADVISORS

The officers and men of the Marine Advisory Unit, who served with the Vietnamese Marine Corps, were a major part of the Marine advisory effort, but there were those (officers and enlisted advisors) who served in a variety of advisory positions, mostly unheralded, with the Naval Advisory Group, MACV, CORDS, and MACV SOG; many assigned to extremely isolated areas that were controlled by the Viet Cong. Much of their work was at the grassroots level, serving with the Vietnamese Regional (RF) and Popular (PF) Forces, which began in 1964, when Major Edward J. Bronars was assigned as the first U.S. Marine Advisor in the Mekong Delta. The enlisted Marine Advisors were the backbone of the Vietnamese counterinsurgency program due to their time in service and their expertise as intelligence, communications, and engineer specialists. U.S. Navy corpsmen served as medical specialists in this phase of the advisory effort.

Vietnamese Marines move on a trail through dense foliage. They are keenly aware, that the "element of surprise" is advantageous to the enemy.

Seacoasts of the delta have extensive mangrove swamps, including the Rung Sat southeast of Saigon, and the U Minh Forest along the west coast; vegetation on the tidal mudflats is dense, root structure is high and tangled, and covering is thick, making access difficult and cross-country movement arduous. Here, Vietnamese Marines use "field expediency" to cross a flooded area; it was necessary to adapt tactics to the lay of the land.

ADVISORY TEAM 43

1968

Chief Journalist R.S. Rose

Ten miles southeast of Saigon, between the capital city and the South China Sea, sits some of the nastiest real estate in South Vietnam. It's the legendary Forest of Assassins—the Rung Sat Special Zone (RSSZ), 400 square miles of swamp, overgrown by NIPA PALM and mangrove, cobwebbed by meandering streams and muddy rivers with twelve-foot tides, which at the ebb barely conceal sunken stumps and shifting sandbars.

In the Rung Sat, the Marines are assigned to a difficult and challenging role: combatant instructors in the most lethally realistic school in the world. They have fought and they have been decorated for their valor; but their principal mission is to train the Vietnamese military forces and advise the military commander of the area.

They are Marine Advisory Team 43, a tightly knit group of three officers, seven enlisted men and their two pet dogs. As part of the Naval Advisory Group, Vietnam, the team operates independently of the other Marine advisory units who work exclusively with Vietnamese Marines.

The team works and lives in a small, one-story, three-room "hootch" in the Vietnamese Regional Forces compound outside the Navy base at Nha Be. The base, 10 miles south of Saigon, is located at the northwestern border of the Rung Sat. It is also the home of three river patrol boat (PBR) sections, a Navy armed helicopter detachment, a Seal unit, an Army communications outfit and a Seabee detachment.

Nha Be is also the headquarters of the commander of the Rung Sat Special Zone, Vietnamese Navy Lieutenant Commander Nguyen An. Because of its geography, the RSSZ is the only land area in South Vietnam under the operational command of the Vietnamese Navy.

Within this set up Marine Advisory Team 43 has a two-fold purpose—to provide specialized advice to Lieutenant Commander An in the fields of infantry, intelligence and political warfare, and to provide assistance in these fields to the senior U.S. Advisor in the Rung Sat, Commander Charles N. Straney.

Because of the close working relationship between the Marines and the senior advisor and his staff, the assistant advisor, Lieutenant Commander, Alvin N. Catalano, also lives at, and works out of, the Marine hootch.

The team works primarily with the 13 Regional Force companies, which comprise a part of Vietnam's home guard. It also provides coordination with visiting U.S., Thai and other Vietnamese forces operating in the area.

The Xung Kich, The Rung Sat commandos, are the product of Marine Advisory Team 43 training. This elite reaction force, the only one of its kind, has become the most efficient fighting force in the Rung Sat. In the ten months of its existence, it has earned a reputation for competence and enthusiasm, which inspired and won the hearts of the residents of the area, while throwing fear into the hearts of the Viet Cong.

Captain David Brown, a 29-year-old, seven-year veteran of the Corps, who serves as the unit's political warfare advisor, heads Marine Advisory Team 43. He is assisted by Staff Sergeant Charles D. Alsbrooks, Jr., and Boatswain's Mate First Class Clayton L. Robinson.

The team's medical advisor, Navy Hospital Corpsmen First Class Harry F. Ladue, works closely with the political warfare section.

Capt. C.R. Dunning (left) and 1st Lt. Vinh Kham discussed an impending ambush operation before leaving Nha Be.

Sgt. James W. May, Jr., took part in an ambush in South Vietnam's Rung Sat Special Zone.

Their job is to advise the Rung Sat commander on psychological warfare, civic action and social welfare—in addition to providing support and advice to Regional Force cultural teams.

"It's a long way from Pennsylvania to the Rung Sat," Captain Brown says, "but people are much the same everywhere, and the soldiers and villagers of the Rung Sat are very friendly and very responsive to our efforts."

The objectives of the political warfare section are all interconnected and designed to build the morale of the Vietnamese forces in the Rung Sat, aid the local populace, and gain support for the government of the Republic of Vietnam by demonstrating that the government is behind the people. This is accomplished, to a great extent, by Captain Brown's traveling cultural team—a combination supply train, camp show, medicine wagon and movie theater. The team is always accompanied by two of the advisors.

Three or four times a month the team moves out, alternately touring the upper and lower sections of the Rung Sat, visiting all of the villages on the circuit.

"These trips have been the highlight of my Vietnam tour," Captain Brown says. "We'll visit three or four villages, distribute wheat, oats, salad oil and other commodities, sing a few songs and move on to the next village."

Transportation from village to village starts out by Vietnamese landing craft, but as the streams grow narrower, the team switches to rented sampans.

"We'll also check with the village chiefs, provincial health representatives and school teachers to see if there's anything special they need. Pencils, writing tablets or light bulbs; if they want them, we'll see what we can do to get them."

The handouts are received from many sources. Much of the food comes from in-country agencies such as the World Health Organization (WHO), Catholic Relief, World Vision, CARE, and USAID. Clothing and soap come from private organizations in the United States such as Masons, fraternal organizations and churches.

In the evening, the site for the overnight stay is reached. A different village hosts the cultural team each night. Here they will set up their generator and get their motion picture projector ready. Then the band will play a few songs.

"I know one Vietnamese song, and I get requests to sing it every time we visit a village." Captain Brown learned to speak Vietnamese through a Marine Corps Institute tape course, fortified by five weeks of language and advisory training at the Army's John F. Kennedy Special Warfare Center at Fort Bragg, North Carolina. Other preparation also included ten weeks of psychological operations training. Captain Brown is the only school-trained psyops officer in the Rung Sat.

The band plays for about an hour. At least 12 of the 17-man Vietnamese section take part in each field trip, and the band members are usually among them. "The band has two electric guitars, violin, a set of drums, and an amplifier and tuner," explains Captain Brown.

Captain Brown's counterpart, Regional Force Second Lieutenant Loc, runs the whole trip. He makes the transportation arrangements as well as the distribution list of clothing and supplies. It is Lieutenant Loc who meets with the village chiefs to discuss problems.

It is also Lieutenant Loc who introduces and explains the movies which are shown. "We have three kinds of movies," Staff Sergeant Alsbrooks explains. "The Vietnamese movies range from the VC and Chicom brutality to ARVN (Vietnamese Army) victory and pacification period. The American movies are educational types, including travelogues, and straight entertainment types. Westerns and slapstick are very popular."

One of the most popular of recent movies was a travelogue on California. Staff Sergeant Alsbrooks remembers, "When those oranges started pouring into the grading machine, everyone cheered when they saw all the fruit."

After the movie, the villagers returned to their homes while the chiefs, the elders, the advisors and Lieutenant Loc sit up to 1 a.m. or later, talking and singing.

But the visits to the villages, colorful though they are, constitute only a small part of Captain Brown's job. He also scouts out civic action projects, drafts, designs and supervises the distribution of leaflets, and assists local people in getting employment at the nearby U.S. Navy base.

The psyops leaflets drafted and designed by Captain Brown are translated by a member of the Vietnamese team and printed by the U.S. Army in Bien Hoa. During one recent month, 301,000 leaflets were dropped in the Rung Sat. Target for the leaflets drops varies from the VC, who are urged to rally to the side of the South Vietnam government, to the population, who are encouraged to report VC activity in their areas. Leaflets contain maps of the Rung Sat to enable potential ralliers to locate Regional Force outposts, newsclips of VC atrocities, and letters from former VC who have joined in support of the South Vietnam Government.

Another area of political warfare is the Medical Civic Action Program (MEDCAP). "Doc" Ladue visits eight villages a month, accompanying a Vietnamese doctor and corpsman. The 33-year-old veteran of 11 years in the Navy observes and advises on treatment. He will occasionally be asked to verify a complicated diagnosis if he can.

As the only medical advisor in the Rung Sat, and the only preventative medicine technician in the Saigon area, he is one of the busiest members of the team.

As Medical Advisor, Ladue has a similar mission to the other advisors—to lessen his Vietnam counterparts' dependence on U.S. medical facilities by training them in diagnosis, treatment, and supply requisitioning through local channels.

Ladue's biggest continuing problem, and one stemming from lack of hygienic practices, is skin disease. This is followed closely by upper respiratory infections. "If I could teach the people how to use soap and water," he says, "we'd have much less trouble with minor cuts and bruises getting infected."

The Rotary Club in his hometown sent 100 pounds of bar soap for the local people. "You can sure see the difference down river," he says, proudly, "where we've distributed both the soap and the know-how."

Cholera has been another recent problem, with three outbreaks since August 1967. During these outbreaks, Ladue and his Vietnamese corpsmen counterparts administered more than 14,000 shots, giving 100 percent coverage in the infected areas.

That the people appreciate the work of the medical and psyops teams is indicated by the increasing frequency with which they cooperate with the Vietnamese troops. Many woodcutters and farmers now refuse to aid the VC, reporting their activities and location to the government forces, and identifying those enemy attempting to infiltrate the villages, carrying out their covert operations.

Analyzing this information received from the people, as well as that received from numerous other sources, is the job of the Rung Sat intelligence squad.

The intelligence advisor to the Rung Sat commander is Captain Edward R. Haines. He is assisted by Staff Sergeant Charles F. Nelch Jr., and Navy Yeoman First Class Kenneth B. Peavy.

The intelligence advisors also assist in training and operational deployment of the Rung Sat intelligence squad. This includes deploying agents to gather intelligence information and coordinating intelligence squad activities with Regional Force reaction units and ambush operations.

As with the other Marine Advisory Team members, Captain Haines serves on

When SSgt Samuel M. Garland (left) and Capt. David Brown aren't taking part in combat operations, they exercise to maintain their high level of readiness.

the staff of the Senior U.S. Advisor, Commander Straney. In this capacity, he provides intelligence assistance to all U.S. military forces in the Rung Sat, as well as to U.S. and allied advisory teams in subsectors adjoining the area.

Information is received from all allied units, including Air Force planes flying over the Rung Sat, river patrol boats (PBRs) and minesweeping boats (MSBs) on the rivers, U.S. Army advisors working in the Rung Sat and adjoining area, and civilians working with the Vietnamese.

They also analyze information gained from Hoi Chanh (former VC who had rallied to the government of the Republic) and prisoners captured by Vietnamese units.

Captain Haines is required to keep track of all enemy activity in the Rung Sat, disseminating intelligence information to U.S. and Vietnamese units going out on ambush and reaction operations, and participating in these operations to gather more information.

Captain Haines also holds weekly conferences with intelligence personnel from adjoining areas.

Staff Sergeant Nelch works directly with the intelligence squad, accompanying them on almost all of their missions. The 32-year-old Californian finds his job interesting and continually challenging. "In the 14 years I've been in the Corps I've had many unusual assignments, but working with the Regional Force troops, as well as with the Americans and the Thai, has given me a scope of experience wider than any I'd ever imagined.

"The challenge, the variety of experience, the people with whom I work—all have combined to make this tour outstanding."

Captain Haines, in the typically cool manner of the traditional intelligence officer, says little, but accomplishes just about everything. He just does his job with the assurance that when the enemy begins a secret operation, it doesn't remain secret for long.

But the enemy also takes a great deal of overt action—direct attacks on merchant ships—because the Rung Sat has one very important strategic value. It surrounds the meandering Long Tau Shipping Channel—four rivers, which wind for 44 miles from the South China Sea to the crowded docks of Saigon.

It has long been the aim of the Viet Cong to sink a ship in the center of the Long Tau and block the river to traffic. Despite over 60 attempts in the last two years, the VC has been significantly unsuccessful.

But when the enemy makes these unsuccessful attempts, he also reveals his location. And when he does, the Vietnamese Regional Force troops in the area are quick to react. Once again, the guiding hand of the MAT 43 Marines is evident.

When a pre-planned operation, a quick reaction operation or an ambush is set up, the political warfare and intelligence sections join the infantry section in the operation. And almost every operation has been an unqualified success, due to the training and advice given by the infantry section.

Heading the infantry section is Captain Clifford R. Dunning. The 29-year-old Naval Academy graduate is assisted by Staff Sergeant Samuel M. Garland and Sergeant James W. May Jr.

The infantry advisor, as with the political warfare and intelligence advisors, has the primary job of advising the Rung Sat commander and the senior U.S. advisor. He helps Lieutenant Commander An prepare for ground operations by offering assistance in tactics and the employment and deployment of troops. He also works with U.S. Army Advisors in the subsectors, and acts as liaison with Army units which come into the Rung Sat from outside the area.

One of the more spectacular accomplishments of the infantry section is the establishment and training of the Rung Sat commandos (Xung Kich), made up of the highest qualified representatives of the 13 Regional Force companies in the Rung Sat Regional Forces. First Lieutenant Vinh Kham heads this elite 25-man platoon.

Vietnamese Regional Force 1st Lt. Vinh Kham (left) and SSgt Samuel Garland discussed ways to teach the Regional Force Commandos (Xung Kich) how to use the lensatic compass properly.

Since its establishment in June 1967, this young, determined, and energetic group has made a name for itself through accomplishments far overshadowing its relative small size. As Staff Sergeant Garland puts it: "There are only 25 men in the platoon, now; yet they accomplish more than companies four times their size."

The primary jobs of the commandos are reaction and ambush. Staff Sergeant Garland and Sergeant May are the advisors who work directly with the group.

They assist in the training, advising and assisting Lieutenant Kham. In many cases such as demolition and communications training, they do the actual instructing while Lieutenant Kham translates.

Captain Dunning attributes the outstanding record of the commandos directly to the two sergeants. "Without Garland and May, the Xung Kich wouldn't be half as effective as they are. We started with the best men and put them under the best instructors, and now we have the best fighting outfit in the Rung Sat."

Staff Sergeant Garland is well trained for the job. In his eight years in the Corps, the 28-year-old Virginian has served for two years as a drill instructor at the Marine Corps Recruit Depot, Parris Island, South Carolina, and supplemented his own excellent Corps training by attending and being graduated from the U.S. Army Ranger School, Fort Benning, Georgia.

Sergeant May has been in the Marine Corps for three years. He serves as communications advisor to the communications sections of the Rung Sat forces.

All three infantry advisors have been decorated for their work with the commandos. These awards include four Bronze Stars with combat "V", two Navy Commendation Medals with combat "V", four Purple Hearts, and three Vietnamese Crosses of Gallantry. Captain Dunning was recently awarded the Silver Star for conspicuous gallantry in action and outstanding leadership under fire. He earned this during one of the commandos' earliest reaction operations, in November 1967. In that action, 15 commandos, eight other Regional Force troops and two Marine advisors were airlifted behind enemy lines, where they killed 23 enemy in a combined effort with air strikes by fixed wing aircraft and gunship helicopters. The target was an estimated company-size Viet Cong unit, which had hit a merchant ship with rocket fire in the shipping channel.

In their spare time, which comes at infrequent intervals, the MAT 43 members relax. But even the relaxation is rugged.

A possible Viet Cong booby trap was pointed out to YN1 Kenneth B. Peavy (left) by Capt Edward R. Haines, the intelligence advisor of Marine Advisory Team 43.

One bit of relaxation taken regardless of workload is the old Marine standby, PT. In addition to using the new weight machine in the Nha Be base gym, the Marines use lifting weights obtained by Captain Dunning. Captain Brown and Staff Sergeant Garland are seen frequently loping along the perimeter of the base, their combat boots sunk deep into the sand, hand-held dumbbells pumping furiously in the breezeless air. They also play their famous "Marine football." Any receiver who misses a pass does ten pushups on the spot.

Another spare-time project is letter writing. They write not only to family and friends but also to churches, clubs and organizations, soliciting donations which can be passed out during MEDCAP and psychological operations trips.

But whether they're relaxing, training themselves or their counterparts, doing pushups, planning ambushes, gathering intelligence information, showing movies to villagers, or shooting it out with "Charlie," the men of the team are always aware that the effectiveness of their work is measured by the success of the Vietnamese whom they advise.

These successes are increasingly evident and as for acceptance by the Vietnamese, Lieutenant Kham, of the commandos describes it.

"They're wonderful men. We think of them not as Americans, not as someone apart from us, but as Vietnamese. We all work together, we all share the same dangers, and we all can get killed together. We are friends."

That feeling of friendship is returned by the Marines. Friendship, acceptance by their Vietnamese counterparts and the overall success of their entire program sum up the mission and accomplishment of U.S. Marine Advisory Team 43.

The Strategic Hamlet Program was part of the South Vietnam's government "pacification" plan where the people living in rural areas would move into self constructed hamlets and provide their own self defense and security. The program did not prove a success due to the lack of government support, the rural peasants indifference to politics (they only wanted to be left alone), and the overall factor that the Viet Cong guerrilla was the root of the local environment; identical to the people and could not be separated from the countryside. The inhabitants of this hamlet work on their defenses under the supervision of armed PFs (Popular Forces). They have built a moat around the hamlet and are putting in punji stakes (sharpened bamboo or other wood stakes) as an outer defense. The Viet Cong also used punji stakes.

TRAGIC MISCALCULATION – A U.S. plane and its tail section fall toward Earth an instant after the craft was severed by an American artillery shell at Na Phan, South Vietnam, in August 1967. This split-second photo was made by UPI photographer Hiromichi Mine. (UPI Telephoto) Chattanooga News-Free Press, Sunday, January 28, 1973.

THE MARINE CORPS AT THE BEGINNING OF ITS FORMATION

Brigadier General Tran Van Nhut

The Marine Corps was formed in 1.10.1954.

1. The first unit had a French name: "Premier Bataillon de l'Infanterie Marine", which was abbreviated to 1er BIM. The battalion was made of a number of Commando Companies that had moved south to Nha Trang after the Geneva Pact. The Battalion Commander was a French Captain by the name of Delayen, who went on to become a general whilst fighting in Chad, Africa. He later retired and moved to America. The Executive Officer was Captain Bui Pho Chi.

2. A company named Corp Franc, commanded by Second Lieutenant Tran Van Nhut, was not part of the 1er BIM, but fell under the orders of the Marine Infantry of the Vietnamese Navy Headquarters in Saigon. Its staff was composed of:

Lieutenant Colonel Le Quang Trong—Commander.

Major Pham Van Lieu—Executive Officer

Captain Nguyen Kien Huong Giang—Chief of S1.

Captain Le Nguyen Khang—Chief of S4.

3. Two Riverine Companies commanded by Captain Nguyen Kien Hung and Captain Khu Duc Hung. These two companies were later dissolved.

Captain Bui Pho Chi became the Battalion Commander in 1955 when Captain Delayen and another American Captain by the name of Breckinridge moved to TRIM Group—a training unit.

In January 1956, Captain Nguy Van Thanh became the Commander of the 1st Marine Battalion. Two Company Commanders at that time were promoted to the rank of General: Major General Bui The Lan and Brigadier General Tran Van Nhut. The Chief of S3 at that time, First Lieutenant Nguyen Ba Lien, also became Brigadier General.

Four platoon leaders became Colonel: Colonel Pham Van Chung, Colonel Ngo Van Dinh, Colonel Do Ky, and Colonel Le Dinh Que.

In April 1956, the Marine Infantry of the Vietnamese Navy changed its name to the Vietnamese Marine Corps of the Navy.

After Lieutenant Colonel Le Quang Trong, the successive Commanders were: Major Pham Van Lieu, Captain Bui Pho Chi, and Major Le Nhu Hung. Each of them commanded the Group for a short period.

From 1960, Captain Le Nguyen Khang became Commander of the Marine Group, which was composed of:

The 1st Marine Battalion, commanded by Captain Tran Van Nhut. The 2nd Marine Battalion, commanded by Captain Nguyen Thanh Yen.

Captain Nguy Van Thanh and his staff, 1956.

A MONTAGE OF WAR

Combat Images of the Vietnamese Marines

TET MAU THAN OFFENSIVE 1968

Major M.C. Tran Xuan Dung

Just after midnight on the eve of the lunar New Year,
Sounds of firearms were heard in nearby Nha Trang.
The civilians wondered what was happening
In the direction of the Naval Training School.

Explosions also occurred in Ban Me Thuot.
Then in Kon Tum, followed by Hoi An,
Pleiku, Danang, Qui Nhon.
And the blood in the civilian homes coloured the green New Year cakes red.

Though it was Tet, the festive mood was no more.
Due to the continuous shooting by the Viet Cong.
And over by the yellow blossom tree,
A now handless girl wept heartachingly.

The Viet Cong had gathered secretly, preparing their attack.
They infiltrated four tactical zones.
They first assaulted in the 2nd Corps
And the following day continued attacking the rest of South Vietnam.

The Viet Cong reached the capital, Saigon.
They had three targets in mind:
The national radio station, the presidential palace
And the U.S. embassy.

Beginning with their firearms,
They then launched B40 rockets.
The palace rear gates were soon destroyed;
Armed with machine guns our guards responded...

Along Nguyen Du Street, they dashed from tree to tree.
Their blood wetted the tree trunks
And their enemy bodies
Littered the street, and their weapons lay scattered.

A car approached the U.S. embassy,
Its occupants fired at the walls,
In the side wall a hole soon gaped,
Through which the enemy tried to charge.

Five U.S. Marines were standing guard,
And fired to defend, to repel.

Major M.C. Tran Xuan Dung, Tet Mau Than Offensive, 1968.

The Viet Cong fell, one by one.

Calm was restored after six hours.

Masquerading in combat police uniforms,

They numbered an entire truckload.

They aimed to occupy

The national radio broadcasting station.

A radio technician was bold

And refused to air the Communists' programs.

Not knowing how to broadcast it themselves,

They vented their frustration on the equipment.

In camouflaged fatigues

The Airborne troops arrived

To change the situation

And soon the invaders' corpses lay scattered in the station.

In Tan Son Nhut Airport,

The enemy approached three battalions at a time.

Attacking simultaneously from East, West and North

Their rockets commencing the attack.

Flares suspended in the sky brightened the spring night,

The airport's minefields could not halt their advance.

Control of the airport teetered

For the outposts were lost and the enemy continued their advance.

Two Airborne Companies of the 8th Battalion,

Demonstrating their well known bravery,

Stopped the enemy advance, fighting well into daybreak.

The Viet Cong withdrew and hid in a nearby textile factory.

Control of the airport now restored,

Helicopters and fighters soon took off

To search and destroy.

The target? The textile factory.

Different places in the capital

The Viet Cong tried to occupy.

They invaded the Joint General Staff Headquarters.

One building was lost, the situation was precarious.

The Viet Cong outnumbered the guards,

And attacked from all sides.

The Marine Task Force B from Cai Lay

Was airlifted back to save Headquarters.

The "Sea Tigers" were tenacious fighters
And reversed the situation within hours.
The NVA's regiment "101"
Withdrew towards the Binh Loi Bridge.

While in Go Vap it just so happened
That the Artillery headquarters was invaded by the enemy.
But the artillerymen removed all essential parts,
So the Viet Cong could not use our canons.

Their attack on the naval base did not meet with success,
They failed to seize the boats moored in the deep,
And their reinforcements could not cross the river.
Defeated, they knew not where to run.

In many districts, the enemy had penetrated deeply.
They searched civilian homes
To kill the relatives of men in uniform
And to shoot all government officials.

In Phu Tho, Racecourse, Bay Hien junction
There was fighting everywhere. In Minh Mang district,
In Cholon, at police stations,
And in Gia Dinh, the trouble lasted for many days.

At Binh Loi Bridge the fighting continued,
Marines were stationed to block both ends.
Two sweltering nights then ensued.
Finally, the Marine Task Force B humbled the Viet Cong.

In Tran Hung Dao Street, black smoke darkened the sky,
For the Viet Cong had burnt civilian homes and their innocent owners too.
The air reeked of the burning smell of human flesh.
As the Marines and police fought back, the enemy moved into the alleyways.

A Viet Cong was caught, and the people were pleased,
Their pity was only for those just killed by him.
His cruelty to innocent civilians made General Loan's blood boil
And he took out his gun to mete out justice.

The Viet Cong's body was flung backwards,
Blood spurted forth from the deadly wound.
All Viet Cong deserve such a death
And first of all, Ho Chi Minh.

New Year's in the Imperial City,
Tinh Tam Lake was blanketed in fog.

127

At three in the morning enemy artillery hammered,
Their 122mm rockets thundered.

The Viet Cong attacked the Perfume River's north bank,
Then they advanced to the west gate of the citadel.
Their battalions assaulted simultaneously,
And managed to cross its thick walls.

The "Black Panthers" were waiting for them
At the east end of the airstrip.
One of the Viet Cong battalions was repelled,
And they retreated in the direction of some houses.

As for the other Viet Cong battalion,
They were occupying a camp
Before being dislodged by the "Black Panthers"
Who now added this to their long list of victories.

Both banks of the Perfume River were in danger,
The city was in enemy claws.
Three regular NVA regiments
Fanned out about the citadel and its environs.

The Viet Cong drove on towards the Imperial Palace,
Which they easily occupied.
Stranded and outnumbered, the First Infantry Division Headquarters
Hung in and braved all enemy fire.

It was impossible to imagine that it was actually Tet,
Given the amount of suffering to which these city dwellers were subjected.
City streets were transformed into battlegrounds,
And white rice cakes were a sticky blood red.

The natives of Hue bore tragic visages,
And one morning, as the heavy fog lifted,
They saw the sight of the Viet Cong's flag adorned with yellow star
Flying above the citadel: it was the harbinger of death.

Around the citadel was a moat,
Inside it, numerous walls,
Interlacing paths and alley ways,
The palace itself, its gardens, and those of the inhabitants.

All this was ideal for hidden troops,
A perfect labyrinthine complexity.
Meanwhile the enemy built trenches and bunkers,
Meanwhile they had not been able to quash the 1st Infantry Division.

The Viet Cong tried to control the citizens.

They opened the prisons, releasing some thousands of criminals.

They persuaded military and government officials to surrender.

Their voices reverberated from megaphones.

The NVA searched each house thoroughly

And shot innumerable inhabitants on the spot.

Those suspected were led away to be tortured,

Death rained down on every household.

The fighting was ceaseless,

The 3rd Regiment was called in to reinforce.

The situation was dangerous, but the morale of the infantrymen remained strong

Meanwhile, the 1st Infantry Division still tried to hold out.

The communists forced the civilians to participate

In all their political propaganda,

Like attending meetings and raising communist's banners,

And spying on each other.

Not all civilians reported to the communists,

Anxious for their destiny, they hid within their homes.

Elderly women were felled by bullets,

Rats nibbled at the swollen corpses of babies.

After controlling Hue for five days

They entered Phu Cam cathedral.

Some hundred Catholics were captured

Until now, where they are buried remains unknown.

People were randomly killed

They stabbed, shot, and decapitated.

Petrified, a woman hid under a staircase

Nursing a dead baby in her arms.

More than half of the Imperial City was brought to its knees,

The ARVN tried to liberate district by district.

The allied forces helped in the southern half,

And all under the depressing drizzly weather.

Schools and homes were shelled,

Flying bullets, and screeching artillery shells rained down.

Torn flesh, bodies flung high,

Stones and bricks fell, bones were crushed.

The 1st Infantry Division was finally reinforced,

And the tide turned in the favor of the ARVN.

Three Airborne battalions: the second, the seventh, and the ninth
Were deployed, and all fought fiercely.

Military corpsmen, aided and medevacuated,
The wounded soldiers gave each other priority in being treated.
All wounds were equally painful, they reasoned,
It was all in the name of serving the nation.

The Imperial Palace long since invaded
Now housed NVA field headquarters.
As it was surrounded by thick strong walls
It posed quite a challenge for the ARVN.

As the dreadful days passed,
Perfume River languished and lost her beauty.
As the southern bank slowly recovered
Displaced people searched for their mothers, mothers looked for their children

The emaciated population—dispirited souls,
Dug and pushed aside bricks and rubble to find family
But only found hair glued fast by blood to scalps and
Bodies so far decomposed, the faces were unrecognizable.

Hoards of rats—overjoyed, ran and
Cried shrilly as they nibbled on the human flesh and bones.
Here and there skulls lay shattered against the walls,
And a New Year banner still dangled from the roof

Meanwhile, Marine Task Force "A"
Battled in close combat within the citadel.
In "tiger-striped" uniforms they stormed,
The flagpole would before long fly another flag.

Saigon under attack, TET 1968.

And then an encouraging piece of news for our fighters:
The NVA field commander had been killed
And with him had died the communists fighting spirit,
And sooner or later the rest of the NVA too would be no longer.

About 100,000 civilians were homeless,
They lived in the ruins of their homes,
Schools and cathedrals were swamped with refugees,
There were no blankets, no rice, but destitution was in abundance.

Ladderless, the Marines still tried to recover the citadel,
Trying to reach the ramparts, they stood on each other's shoulders,
Under the rain of enemy fire, their battle cries reverberated.
The flagpole was heroically recaptured.

Enemy bodies, torn and a slippery red lay like litter,
A mélange of skin, bones, earth and bricks.
The survivors fled to Van Thanh,
In the now damaged city of Hue, the noise of firearms finally ceased.

Brigadier General Ngo Quang Truong had been awaiting the moment
To demand that his men raise the flag,
The "Sea Tigers" were surprised by such an inappropriate request,
But to bicker seemed so trivial, and the Brigadier's will was done.

Flinging their weapons high, the fighters shouted for joy,
The gun smoke had not yet cleared,
But the communist flag had already been lowered
To be torn and trampled underfoot.

Everyone waited with baited breath for that moment
When the South Vietnamese flag was jubilantly raised.
Its brilliant yellow hue flapped in the breeze,
The soldiers cheered, the civilians shouted in happiness.

But tears still streamed...
People looking hopelessly for family still,
Discovering instead the mass graves
Of those massacred by the NVA.

An elderly woman stood by the grave—her legs buckled
When she caught sight of her child as the bodies were unearthed.
Someone leapt in, catching sight of something familiar.
Another clasped the shoe of a loved one and wept.

The bodies lay, indifferent to the cries and shouts
They lay in different positions; but they had all met with the same fate

Relatives tried to identify them,
Some succeeded, others ironically not so "lucky".

6,000 innocents slaughtered
Some lay crumpled, others fully extended.
One corpse lay legless,
Others boasted crushed skulls, swollen abdomens full of maggots.

5,000 of the enemy had been killed,
But somehow the butchering of innocent civilians overshadowed this fact.
But in the eyes of the civilians, before their anger be somewhat alloyed,
Revenge should be visited upon the enemy at least ten-fold.?

The ARVN also suffered losses for the nation,
400 had laid down their lives,
1,800 had been wounded,
To save the civilians, to gain victory.

In the Mau Than Offensive,
The enemy had attacked the four tactical zones in the same way,
Commencing first by shelling with artillery,
They backed this up with the advance of their regular and sapper units.

A hundred thousand homes destroyed,
41 cities attacked,
Ten of them severely damaged,
Civilian deaths too high...

The grief unfolded for the
14,000 civilians killed,
And for the heartbreaking condition of the wounded,
Who numbered a painful 25,000

TET -1968. Viet Cong Commandos lay dead amid the rubble of the fighting in Cholon – Chinese quarter of Saigon – as refugees flee; the attacks began after midnight on 31 January 1968. Throughout Vietnam the Communists had launched their attacks on Tet – the Lunar New Year – the most important of all the Vietnamese holidays; over 40,000 enemy troops were killed. Note the uniform and rocket launcher on one of the dead.

Captain John F. Stennick, US Marine Advisor, hands out clothing to widows of Vietnamese Marines killed in combat. He is assisted by a female captain (Vietnamese Marine social welfare officer) in camouflage uniform with VNMC insignia. Captain Stennick's wife was instrumental in starting a church drive in the U.S. to collect the clothing.

THE WIFE OF A MARINE

Mrs. Nguyen Van The

I lived side by side with the Sea Tigers from 1964 to the day our country fell to the red devils. Though I was never at the frontlines, I understood the mentality of the Marines, and shared their joys as well as their hardships. My most vivid memories are of the time they returned from Laos, and when they moved to Hue. I was part of a group of singers who were going to La Vang church to entertain and welcome the "Sea Tigers" back from Laos. I was so very happy to see my husband and friends again. The ARVN had been badly shaken by the outcome of the Laos incursions, and the Marines were also affected. But fortunately, I did not lose too many friends.

Not long after they returned, the situation in the battlefields turned serious again. The whole division went into operation. The night before they left, nobody could sleep. They were so busy packing and preparing. The members of the Marine Medical Battalion, had to pack all sorts of medical equipment and drugs in addition to their weapons. The entire battalion was a hive of activity. Some were impatient to depart; others were painfully tearing themselves from their families.

At 2:00 a.m., everything was ready. As wives of the Marines, we were allowed to gather at the camps courtyard, to bid them farewell. We watched the trucks carrying our loved ones approach our position in cloud of dust illuminated eerily by the headlights. It was the first time I had witnessed them leave at night. The convoy rumbled past us. First came the 1st Marine Battalion, then the second... my husband was in the 4th Battalion. I watched the truck carrying the "Sea Tigers" go by—they looked so calm, sitting there clutching their weapons and heavy rucksacks, ready to stare fate in the face. They were determined to carry out their duties as Sons of the South by ensuring freedom and peace for our country. Few people were privileged as myself to witness their quiet and personal sacrifices. It was very emotional to watch them leave, and I recalled a poem about a fighter's wife we had learned at school:

"The filtered water under the bridge was clear and the road by the bridge was green with grass. Broken-hearted, I bid farewell to my beloved...."

At that moment, I felt a strong bond of sisterhood with all the wives and lovers of the fighters. We women lived in perpetual fear of bad luck. Our eyes flooded regular inundated by tears of hope and agony for our men. Every time an operation was organized, we prepared ourselves for the losses that were sure to come. But all we could do was pray.

The convoy took them to Phan Thanh Gian Bridge, to await further transportation to the air base. Six months later, I was allowed to fly to Hue. I dressed myself in tiger-striped fatigues, and accompanied a logistical team that was heading to the front lines to re-supply the Marines.

I arrived at the Division Headquarters at 3:00a.m. The convoy arrived at the air base at 4:00a.m. But it wasn't until 1:00 PM the next day that we were able to board a C130 aircraft to fly to Hue. The aircraft landed at Phu Bai airfield. As we alighted, we saw that the tarmac was alive with "Sea Tigers". Some had newly arrived, and others were on their way home. The newcomers were healthy, complete in body and were enthusiastic and loud. The returning Marines were riddled with wounds and bore their pains in silence. No pen could possibly describe their agony!

From the air base, we were moved to Small Mang Ca, where the Hue District Hospital was situated. On my way to the Marine Medical Battalion, I had to pass a mortuary. It was a field morgue—bodies were laid in ponchos, on tables, and coffins... I was deeply moved. Tears ran down my face. I thought of the poor women who were about to receive the horrible news of their beloved. I felt helpless, as there was nothing I could do for these heroes.

When I returned to Saigon, I went to the church of Maria Fatima to pray for the souls of the dead Marines, and asked one of my Aunts to burn incense in memory of the Buddhist souls. It was the least we could do for those fearless souls. I also organized groups to visit and comfort wounded Marines in Saigon and Hue. We wanted to express our gratitude to the fighters who were protecting us, our children, and our nation.

Even after 20 years away from my country, I still remember my days in the Marine base camp. I remember the sisterhood of Marine wives, who followed the progress of their loved ones with trepidation. Dear Marines! When I think of you, I still see heroism and the ravages of war stamped forever more on your noble faces.

THE WHITE-HAIRED OLD MAN

Colonel Ton That Soan

Whenever the nickname "White-Haired Old Man" was mentioned, everyone in the Marines immediately knew who it was. Many of our brothers-in-arms had nicknames, for example, Hai Chua, Chau Phuoc Hiep...etc. But everybody spoke of the "White-Haired Old Man" with respect and affection.

He was Colonel Nguyen Thanh Yen, Assistant Commandant of the Vietnamese Marine Division. He was born in Dalat, and graduated from the Dalat National Military Academy.

He first served in the Airborne Division, fighting in North Vietnam. In 1954, he followed his unit to the South.

In 1956, he volunteered to be transferred to the Marines, which had been formed from elements of the riverine forces of the navy, army commandos who came from the North before 1954, and army commandos of the South.

The 2nd Marine Battalion was formed in Rach Dua, Vung Tau. It then moved to Cam Ranh to be equipped, trained, and receive manpower from Marine recruit posts.

First Lieutenant Yen became Commander of the 2nd Marine Battalion around 1959.

He was a true soldier at heart, and always executed his orders and fulfilled his tasks. He had unlimited enthusiasm for the Nationalist cause, the ARVN, and the Marine Corps. He was open, and straightforward. He never used tricks or maneuvers to harm anybody. He never did anything for his own private gain, although he had a large family—a wife and ten children.

He loved his subordinates like his own brothers. Occasionally, when confronted with some undisciplined soldiers, he had the habit of using his right hand to pass over his short white hair, and queried them with short sentences. Huh? Huh? He used to grunt threateningly as he prodded them with his elbow. Being of short stature, he sometimes fell down as he administered the prodding. Invariably he would laugh, get up, and embrace the soldier. Once his anger was over, he never held a grudge. Because of this habit, he was also dubbed "Old Huh".

In the Marine Corps, he was not only liked because of his openness but also respected for his enthusiasm for the Nationalist cause, ARVN and honor of Marine Corps in the initial stages of the war against the Communist North Vietnam.

I recall clearly the campaign which the V.C. had boasted as a "Simultaneous

A relaxing moment – this young Marine gets a "break" during a field operation. The Vietnamese could savor a rest, a bite of food, or a comical instance, even in the most trying conditions; an art that most Americans failed to master. The patch on his right sleeve identified him as a member of the VNMC 2nd Battalion (Crazy Buffalos).

Upheaval" in Kien Hoa in 1960. In reality, it was a simple event: undercover Communist cadres forces of women and children would go to the market of Giong Trom suburb, District of Mo Cay to demonstrate against the South Vietnamese Government.

The Marine Group, commanded by Major Le Nhu Hung received orders from the Joint General Staff to send the 2nd Marine Battalion to deploy. They were to keep the security in the suburb of Giong Trom and to protect the route leading to Truc Giang City (Kien Hoa) and the 1st Marine Battalion commanded by the First Lieutenant Tran Van Nhut, was to keep security in Mo Cay suburb and the route leading to the Truc Giang City.

During this period, there were only skirmishes at squad level. Marine Companies changed their tactics to disperse very thinly to be able to Search and Destroy the enemy and, at the same time, gather information.

First Lieutenant Yen ordered several soldiers to wear civilian plain clothes and masquerade as motorbike drivers or Xe loi drivers (a "xe loi" is a motorbike which has a passenger box in the back). They were to carry civilians to Giong Trom market, to Binh Dai District, Ba Tri District or Truc Giang City, so they could gather information about enemy activities from them.

Not all these soldiers were accustomed to driving xe lois. A couple of accidents occurred on bumpy roads, sending the driver and passenger headlong into the ditches. Luckily, no one died or was severely injured.

One night, the whole unit was entertained. First Lieutenant Yen had the idea of trying to drive a xe loi himself. I had to intervene several times. (At this stage, I was Executive Officer of the 2nd Battalion.)

His drinking capacity was also very high. When the alcohol impregnated his blood, the sky was no limit. I was his equal, but I always restrained myself to be in control of the situation.

His subordinates, the Company Commanders, were Minh, nicknamed Emile, First Lieutenant Nguyen Van Khai, First Lieutenant Do Ky, and Chief of S3.

Others included:

Master Sergeant Chung Van Nghiem

Master Sergeant Loc

Master Sergeant Minh

Master Sergeant Thach Xut

Master Sergeant Son Xil

Staff Sergeant Nguu

Staff Sergeant Thi

Corporal La Kum, whose hand was so strong that he once strangled a moderate size hog to death.

They were audacious and experienced—most had been from the Commando units in the North, Center and South of Vietnam. Others were soldiers from religious sects. The more I lived with them, the more I liked them. They were absolutely anti-Communist, which was a very cohesive sentiment in the unit. They were proud to wear a green beret and the special fatigues of the Marines, the printed design of which was reminiscent of waves hitting the seashore. During this period, the situation at Mo Cay District where the 1st Marine Battalion was in charge, was rather troublesome. During a search for the enemy in a coconut forest, the squad led by Master Sergeant Pham Khac Dat was ambushed by the enemy. The VC had dug holes, had hidden themselves in them, and covered the tops with a net camouflaged with leaves and hay. When our soldiers marched pass, they leapt out and attacked with scimitars and bayonets. This tactic was known as "don tho". The Marine Squad fought back courageously, quashed the ambush, conserving all weapons. But unfortunately, Master Sergeant Dat was killed in action. A few others were wounded.

In his memory, the Marine Corps named the 1st Marine Battalion's camp in Rung Cam, Thu Duc, after his name. It was the first camp to be named after a slain hero. Later, the camp of the Amphibious Support Battalion carried the name of Major Nguyen Van Nho. The street stretching from that battalion to Thi Nghe market was also named after him. Major Nho was killed in action in the battle of Binh Gia, Phuoc Tuy Province.

Ap Bac and Binh Gia were two big battles at that time.

First Lieutenant Chau, a.k.a "Chau Phuoc Hiep", Commander of the 3rd Company/1st Marine Battalion was with his men performing activities at Mo Cay. Angered with the 'don tho' tactics of the enemy, he sent troops to 'Search and Destroy' instructing that they avoid confrontation, and First Lieutenant Chau earned his nickname.

Officers in the 1st Marine Battalion at that time was composed of:

Executive Officer, First Lieutenant Le Van Hien

Company Commanders:

First Lieutenant Hoang Tich Thong

First Lieutenant Nguyen Thanh Tri

First Lieutenant Le Hang Minh

Chief of S3, Second Lieutenant Vo Van Vuong

There were many other excellent officers.

After two months recruiting in the region recovered, the Marine Group left Kien Hoa for Cuu Long Delta. Major Le Nhu Hung was appointed by President Ngo Dinh Diem as Chief Secretary of Military Affairs. Major Hung transferred his position to Captain Le Nguyen Khang.

First Lieutenant Yen received orders to move his battalion to reinforce the District of Camau to protect the formation and building of "Prosperous Areas"—especially the one in Cai Nuoc, which had been organized by Father Nguyen Lac Hoa. Because it was a large area, and the enemy was still weak, the battalion headquarters positioned at the city and only the companies spread out into areas of responsibility to performed activities. There was no artillery and air power support. The Second Company of First Lieutenant Hai Chua was in charge of recruiting for Father Hoa's prosperous area. The Third Company of First Lieutenant Co Tan Tinh Chau, was stationed at Cai Bat 15km south of the prosperous area.

This was the important 'throat' situated between Cai Bat River and Bay Hap River. The only means of communication and transportation was via civilians' sampans.

Although they carried out separate operations in different areas, all companies were always ready to support each other. A field battalion staff led by myself was positioned with the 3rd Company to coordinate maneuvers. This was an isolated, sparsely populated area without any government regional troops. The enemy was free to do whatever they liked. After a month, there were no skirmishes except for the odd gunshot from the V.C., or the sound of propaganda from their megaphones echoing throughout the hamlets.

Then bad luck struck the battalion Commander.

The Bravo Command Group received a telegram saying, the next morning that the Battalion Commander would come with the Military Financial Group to visit and pay companies at Cai Nuoc. The next morning, First Lieutenant Yen, his escorts, and the Military Treasury (led by Gunnery Sergeant Phat) boarded a sampan. The group, totally 10 in number, was armed with personal weapons (carbine, garant Ml), and a light BAR machine gun.

The boat left the small port in Camau, sailed along Bay Hap River, then Cal Bat River, and finally reached the 3rd Company's position at 11 am. The 3rd Company cleared the road and kept security of the 15km river, while groups of threes from the 2nd Company used sampans to reach the location of the Military Financial Group to receive their monthly salary and to sign a money order for their families. After that, they changed with the 3rd Company. With a distance of 15km, a company could not possibly exert effective control.

At 3:00pm, First Lieutenant Yen and the Military Financial Group returned by the same boat to the mouth of the Bay Hap to get back to Ca Mau.

An hour later, the sound of gunfire came in the direction of Cal Bat. The platoon midway along the road reported via radio that after the boat had passed them, gunfire was heard barely fifteen minutes later—and that the platoon was on its way to the rescue.

The enemy force was also about one platoon. They had investigated the terrain and had known the timing of the Military Financial Group's visit. The leak had come from the Marines, who inadvertently told the civilians they were mixing with, of the visit.

At the curve of the river, the boat had had to slow down, and it was at that moment that the enemy struck. The pilot was injured, and lost control of the boat. It crashed onto the banks of the river. First Lieutenant Yen and his soldiers had no time to react. Sitting in the boat, they were easy targets —the sides were made of wood, offering no protection. Gunnery Sergeant Phat and two other Marines were killed. First Lieutenant Yen was shot in the chest, sending blood spurting everywhere. He audaciously fired back at the enemy with his pistol, making a good show of his calmness to encourage the soldiers to follow suit. In the next wave of attack, three VC leapt aboard. The first VC for some bizarre reason, did not carry a rifle, but instead held a string of exploding firecrackers. Before the other two had fully succeeded in jumping on, the Marine reinforcement platoon arrived and opened fire. Fearing that they might hit their brothers in the boat, they shot at the riverbank as they charged the situation. The enemy, surprised, ran away.

Review of the skirmish found that Gunnery Sergeant Phat and two soldiers were dead, three others were wounded, and First Lieutenant Yen was severely injured in the chest. Weapons were conserved, as was the safe and the letters the Marines had written to their families. The enemy had managed to grab a rucksack as they were leaving.

At that time, there was no such thing as medevac by helicopter. The only way was by sampan or motorized boats; the first was slow, the second was quicker. The Marines did not have a motorized boat of their own, so, we had to hire one. Luckily, a motorized boat came from the direction of the mouth of the Bay Hap River; Gunnery Nghiem stopped it and asked for transportation to Ca Mau. It reached there at 10:00 pm. The unit truck was there, waiting to transport the wounded to the civilian hospital in the city.

The road was 1km long—bumpy, full of potholes that caused the chest wound of First Lieutenant Yen to bleed profusely. Fortunately, he reached the hospital in time to receive treatment.

Later, the district S2, which was gathering information on enemy activities, revealed that the enemy had planned to masquerade as his relatives to enter the hospital to assassinate him. Fortunately, they missed their chance. He had already been transferred to Can Tho Hospital for further treatment, after which he was sent to the Military General Hospital in Saigon.

Not long after his recovery, he wanted to rejoin the unit. Everybody welcomed him warmly, as if he was an elder brother coming home from a long trip. After that, the unit went on to gain victory after victory, and the "White-Haired Old Man" was always present with them.

At Dam Doi, the 2nd Marine Battalion gained victory in 1962—an achievement that was incorporated into our Marine march song. Dam Doi district had been besieged by the enemy, and the 2nd Battalion managed to break their encirclement, seizing a cache of personnel weapons and a collective SKZ made in China.

In the Coup of November 1, 1963, the Coup organizers kept Captain Yen in the Joint General Staff Headquarters with Colonel Cao Van Vien and many other officers, fearing that they would not comply. They knew that Captain Yen was a true soldier at heart, a Catholic who never wanted to involve himself in politics. After the political situation was normalized again, Captain Yen returned to become commander of the Task Force B, and later went on to become Assistant Commandant of the Marine Division.

In any position, he was always in the thick of the battle. He was present at many battles, from the conquest of the Fulro Group in Ban Me Thuot, to the big confrontations at Pleime Duc Co, Bong Son, Phu Cu, Tam Quan, Doi Muoi, and Mang Yang Pass. At Mang Yang, the Marines had to endure cold foggy nights for long periods to protect the population from Qui Nhon to Pleiku.

Bunyo Ishikawa, a Japanese war correspondent, working for Newsweek at that time, wrote several reports and took several photos, praising the Marine units and their commanders. Once, a photo of Lieutenant Colonel Nguyen Thanh Yen with General Westmoreland and other officers made the front page under the caption: *Field Commanders in the Vietnam War.*

In 1966, in the "Central Vietnam Buddhist Rebellion", the Marine Brigade led by Lieutenant Colonel Yen, the 1st Marine Battalion led by Major Ton That Soan, and the 2nd Marine Battalion commanded by Major Le Hang Minh, were sent to re-establish social order and political security. He and Lieutenant Colonel Bui The Lan were both promoted to Colonel in this occasion.

At the beginning of 1970, he left the Marine Corps and was transferred to Quang Da Special District to take the position of Operational Assistant to 1st Corps Commander, Lieutenant General Hoang Xuan Lam.

Early in 1971, he was demobilized. He lived in a house with an orchard next to a canal. It was also the home of his brother-in-law, Colonel Nguyen Van Hiep of the Ranger Group. They had married into the same family. One day, he drowned in the canal, leaving behind many friends, family members and brothers-in-arms to mourn him.

Time passed, our country fell into a miserable state...people dispersed all over the world, and most of the South Vietnamese Army troops were in Communist concentration camps.

Now in free countries, we all try to keep in touch with our brothers-in-arms. Such reunions bring forth a mixture of sadness and happiness. All the memories are resurrected—even the ones 40 years ago are recounted in detail. Geographic names such as Cai Bat, Nam Can, Cai Nuoc, and Dam Doi are mentioned. And of course, the "White Haired Old Man" is remembered with love and respect.

Even though the stars might move and the environment may change, the hearts of the Marines never do.

It moves me every time. I think of the eternal bond between the Marines. The same strong sentiments made me write these lines—a brief eulogy of Colonel Nguyen Thanh Yen, which reflects the mutual feelings we Marines have for the "White Haired Old Man."

"The Vietnamese Marine Spring Victory Exposition," commemorating the Tet Offensive, 1968 (Tet Mau Than). Center photo: The deputy commander, Political Warfare Corps and the Chief of Staff, Vietnamese Marines "cut the tape" at the opening ceremony.

Dân chúng nô-nức kéo nhau đến xem số chiến-lợi-phẩm do Binh-Chủng Mũ Xanh tịch thu của Cộng-quân sau khi đánh tan chúng tại Cố-Đô và Thủ-Đô.

Vietnamese civilians, observing the Communist equipment and weapons captured by the Marines during the battles of Saigon and Hue.

TAI CÔNG-TRƯỜNG LAM-SƠN, PHÓ TỔNG-THỐNG
VNCH TUYÊN-DƯƠNG CÔNG-TRẠNG TẬP-THỂ CHO
CÁC QUÂN, BINH-CHỦNG QLVNCH HỮU CÔNG TRONG
CUỘC DẸP LOẠN CỘNG-SẢN HỒI TẾT MẬU-THÂN.

Phó Tổng-Thống và Đại-Tướng
Tổng Tham-Mưu-Trưởng QLVNCH duyệt binh.

Phó Tổng-Thống VNCH gắn huy-chương cấp Quân-Đội
cho hiệu kỳ Binh-Chủng TQLC.

Trung-Tướng Tổng Trưởng Quốc-
Phòng gắn huy-chương cấp Quân-
Đội cho một chiến-sĩ hữu công.

Đại-Tướng Tổng Tham-Mưu Trưởng
QLVNCH gắn huy-chương cấp Sư-
Đoàn cho một chiến-sĩ TQLC.

Trung-Tướng Tư-Lệnh TQLC ân-
thưởng một Cọp-Biển gan-dạ.

Top two photos: Vice-President Nguyen Cao Ky, inspects the troops and awards an army level award – attached to the flag – to the Marine Division. Bottom three photos: (left to right) Vietnamese Defense Minister, ARVN Chief of Staff, and the Deputy Commander, Vietnamese Marines as they decorate individuals for actions of valor.

141

BUỔI LỄ GẮN HUY-CHƯƠNG CHO CÁC HIỆU KỲ TĐ1 - TĐ4 - TĐ5/TQLC
VÀ CÁC QUÂN-NHÂN HỮU CÔNG TRONG CUỘC HÀNH-QUÂN DIỆT TRỪ GIẶC
CỘNG TẠI CỐ-ĐÔ HUẾ.

Trung-Tướng Tư-Lệnh TQLC duyệt-binh.

Lễ chào Quốc và Quân kỳ trước sân cờ BTL/TQLC.

... Cho hiệu kỳ Tiểu-Đoàn 1/TQLC và Thiếu-Tá PHAN-VĂN-THẮNG.

... hiệu kỳ Tiểu-Đoàn 4/TQLC và Thiếu-Tá ĐỖ-ĐÌNH-VƯỢNG.

iểu-Đoàn 5/TQLC

... Cùng các Chiến-sĩ hữu công.

"Awards Ceremony" at the Marine Headquarters – 1st, 4th and 5th Battalions decorated for their valiant combat at the city of Hue.

Trận đánh sôi động tại Cầu Phan-Thanh-Giản
Trại gà Thanh-Tâm và Xóm Canh-nông thị-nghè

Bloody Battles

VIETNAMESE MARINE COMMANDERS AND STAFF OFFICERS

Lieutenant General Le Nguyen Khang Commandant of the Vietnamese Marine Corps, 1960-1972

Major General Bui The Lan Commandant of the Vietnamese Marine Corps, 1972-1975

Brigadier General Nguyen Ba Lien Was shot down whilst flying overhead in a helicopter during a battle in 1969. Holding the rank of Major he was the Chief of Staff of the Marine Corps, before becoming a Colonel and Commander of Special Zone "24". He was promoted posthumously.

Brigadier General Tran Van Nhut At that time a Major, he was also the Assistant Commandant and Chief of Staff of the Marine Brigade, 1963-64.

Colonel Nguyen Thanh Yen Assistant Commandant of the Vietnamese Marine Division, 1969.

Colonel Nguyen Thanh Tri Assistant Commandant of the Vietnamese Marine Division, 1972.

"THE CHIEF SINEW OF WAR IS THE SPIRIT OF THE ARMY"

—*Tolstoy*

Colonel Hoang Tich Thong
Commander of the 147th Marine Brigade,
1970.

Colonel Ton That Soan
Commander of the Marine Brigade "B,"
pictured in 1968 when he held the rank of
Lieutenant Colonel. The photograph was
taken at Thu Duc after he successfully led
Task Force "B" in a counter attack against
the Communists who had invaded a
number of districts of Saigon.

Colonel Pham Van Chung
Commander of the 369th Marine Brigade,
who successfully halted the NVA advance
at My Chanh River, 1972.

Colonel Ngo Van Dinh
Commander of the 258th Marine Brigade,
1972.

Colonel Nguyen Nang Bao
Commander of the 147th Marine Brigade,
1972.

Colonel Nguyen The Luong
Became the Commander of the 369th
Marine Brigade in May 1972. He is
pictured here as a Lieutenant Colonel.

Colonel Le Dinh Que
Chief of Staff of the Marine Division, 1972.

USMC Vietnamese Marine Advisor Exhibit, Marine Corps Museum; Depicts the advisor, his uniform, and articles used during his tour of duty.

TECHNIQUES OF ADVISING

Introduction

How does the advisor give advice? Each person must find the methods, which will produce results. Varying circumstances and personalities make it impossible to establish a rigid set of rules. This document has been prepared to give an insight into the complex job of Marine Advisor/diplomat. It represents the views, opinions, and recommendations of a number of experienced and successful Marine Advisors. It is offered as guidance to new advisors.

It must be assumed that an officer assigned to the Marine Advisory Unit has broad experience and professional competence for this is the basic foundation for success. Upon reporting to the unit, the advisor should arm himself with as much information as possible concerning his duties. This can be accomplished by means of the "Job Description" provided by the Marine Advisory Unit, thorough briefing by the officer whom he is replacing—if possible, and a detailed study of all applicable directives concerned with duty in the Military Assistance Command, Vietnam.

Upon joining the Vietnamese Marine Battalion, the advisor should initially listen and observe closely. Until he begins to feel that he knows completely what is happening and why, suggestions should not be offered unless asked. He should remember that there have been many Americans before him, and his counterpart probably feels that he knows how to handle advisors. This will be the advisor's first—and probably last—experience of this nature; the Vietnamese experience this change constantly with the rotation of advisors.

General

The relationship between the advisor and counterpart must be based on the solid ground of competent professional knowledge, a mutual respect of services, and if possible, friendly personal contacts. The amalgamation of these will give best results. The advisor should at all times be himself, and not adopt a "new face" for dealings with his counterpart. The manner of extending advice or offering suggestions depends upon personalities, moods and the situation. It has been found that using the same methods one would use to recommend a change of action to an American commander produces excellent results with the Vietnamese commander. Quick changes are not to be expected and every effort should be made to continue the programs of the previous advisor, so that a continuity of programs and aims is apparent. The advisor should work from the "soft sell", with a gradual but persistent approach, featuring repetition of ideas and proposals. It is common, however, that the counterpart will not consider the new arrival as "his advisor" until the two have been exposed to combat together. The new advisor must have patience.

The advisor's goal: To develop a genuine friendship and personal loyalty to his counterpart which will not interfere with the advisor's professional relationship with the counterpart or his objectivity to his job.

Assistance to the Unit

Since advisory duties involve all aspects of the battalion with which the advisor will work, the advisor will find that he must extend his influence through all levels of the command including the senior staff noncommissioned officers. It will often be necessary to give recommendations to, tutor, and encourage the staff officers as well as the company and platoon commanders. This must be done openly with no inference of usurping the battalion commander's authority. Generally, the commander will welcome such assistance.

The advisor must show interest in all facets of battalion operations and training, not solely the activities in which the battalion commander is directly concerned. The advisor must get out and look around, being alert to new practices or new procedures. He must talk to company commanders, platoon commanders, staff officers, and noncommissioned officers, learning their names and their interests. Only in this way will the advisor obtain a feel for the entire battalion. It will also help him know what is going on at all levels of command within the unit. The advisor should also take an interest in the dependents.

The following are considered basic methods of approach:

—Retain a sense of humor. There are many occasions during the advisor's tour where a sense of humor will be a necessity—and an advantage. The Vietnamese are happy people and like to laugh, sometimes in situations which might be considered under strange and morbid circumstances. It is not proposed that the advisor join a crowd in appreciation of the particular effect artillery has on the human body, but neither can he afford to be appalled if the Vietnamese show such an interest. But the advisor can expect to have some embarrassing moments—losing his footing in a tidal stream, reacting too quickly and violently to an incoming mortar round—and the Vietnamese will think that this is hilarious. At a time like this, the only thing the advisor can do is laugh at himself with them.

—Always remember that the counterpart is the commanding officer. It is more practical for an advisor to proffer a suggestion prior to a commander's decision than it is to try to change a decision once it has been made. If there is any one point to be considered absolute doctrine, this is the one. And it behooves the advisor to be alert to anticipate decisions through circumstances and make his suggestions accordingly. The commander can then gracefully accept the advice by appearing as though it was his idea in the first place.

—Do not outwardly display displeasure or disagreement with decisions which have ignored the advice of the advisor. The advisor must make a decision on his own as to whether to fight for his principles, or to save his ammunition for another time, another place, a more important battle. Usually, the advisor finds it advantageous to wait. There have been many instances where the commander, realizing that the advice was good, has reversed himself on his own volition. Further prodding by the advisor would have had the reverse effect of setting the commander's decision irrevocably. The advisor will find that demonstrations and examples will show the relative effectiveness of advisor ideas as compared with existing methods, and changes will eventually result.

—Never boast or attempt to take credit for practices or procedures which are implemented. The fact that the counterpart knows that the original idea was the advisor's is enough credit. This, too, is a vitally important point.

—Set a personal example of dress, bearing, industry, and initiative. The advisor must strive to be professionally correct and military in appearance at all times. The Vietnamese expect a U.S. Marine to be the epitome of strength, endurance, appearance, courage, and military skill. Though the advisor will seldom be aware of this, the Vietnamese will often compare their "Co Van" with those of other Americans serving with the ARVN. The Marine advisor must not let them down.

—Try to visit with U.S. Marine units. The counterpart and his battalion are proud of the fact that they are Marines. When possible, the advisor should make an attempt to take his counterpart to visit a U.S. Organization. With a little assistance and briefing by the advisor, the USMC Commander can give the full VIP treatment to the counterpart, thus increasing his prestige. The visit also provides live training aids for programs in sanitation, staff functioning, unit training, etc., which the advisor may be suggesting. The advisor will be surprised at the many practices that a Vietnamese battalion staff will adapt after they have watched a USMC battalion staff go through its paces.

Headquarters of Vietnamese Marine Corps and US Marine Advisory Effort, Saigon.

—Understand the Vietnamese view. Usually, it is drastically different. But the advisor must realize that a valid suggestion cannot be accepted unless he understands the Vietnamese reason for doing something the way they have been doing it for years. The suggested changes have to be made with a view towards customs and circumstances.

—Give the counterpart time to think over a suggestion. The advisor must learn to offer new ideas or suggest new procedures sufficiently in advance of the need. He will sometimes find that a recommendation given yesterday is being put into practice tomorrow.

—Never lose your temper. This is a sign of weakness and must be avoided. It is permitted to be angry, but the advisor must retain control of his temper. This is not to suggest that occasionally a display of irritation is not appropriate. The advisor will often be irritated, but he must retain his composure most of the time. If a discussion becomes heated and the basic idea is being lost, the best idea is to forget it.

—Trivialities must not become unbearable. The advisor will find that many inconveniences are an inherent part of the advisor tasks, just grin and bear it.

—When deployed, a USMC Advisor will spend about all of his time with the battalion. Advice offered during normal conversation, such as mealtime or during a break, allows the pros and cons of the suggestion to be discussed without the pressure of an immediate decision. The question and answer game also works. By asking questions, you can discover what the counterpart is thinking. Remind him of items which he may have forgotten. He can answer questions and give orders as though he were going to do it that way all along. And the job can be done before the break is over and the advisor can check.

—The advisor must be patient, persistent, and considerate. If the counterpart has demonstrated himself to be a competent leader, it then becomes the advisor's task to build the counterpart's confidence of his subordinates. By being selective in the problems to tackle, the advisor can help the counterpart achieve results which will encourage him to go on to bigger problems.

—Requests will be received by advisors for purchases from the U.S. Exchange services. If the advisor honors one request, it will engender countless other requests. The best way out of the situation is to quote the Exchange regulations. A bonafide gift under special circumstances may be warranted, but that should be the extent of the involvement.

—The "buddy system" or mutual admiration society in lieu of a sound professional basis and sincere personal respect is highly undesirable and offers no advantages.

—The Vietnamese system of officer-enlisted relationship and methods of inflicting commanding officer's punishment is very much different than what the advisor will be accustomed to. The advisor is cautioned not to intercede in any way. He should just try to understand this system—not change it.

Conclusion

The success of the advisor's efforts to win the respect and the cooperation of his Vietnamese counterpart is the direct equation of professional competence and knowledge multiplied by the amount of time that the advisor and counterpart spend together. In other words, the platform for a lasting and firm relationship is built slowly upon solid blocks of good advice. The officers of the Vietnamese Marine Corps are trained, experienced, and proud. The advisor, accordingly, should not expect his counterpart to come to him seeking advice. The advisor should be there, when he is needed, with an encouraging word, a possible recommendation, and enthusiastic support of the commander's eventual order. The patient but persistent advisor who hears his counterpart ask, "What do you think?", has just been informed that he is a success.

"It is their war, and you are to help them, not win it for them."

—Lawrence of Arabia
The Arab Bulletin, 20 August 1917

Vietnamese Marine radio operator, set strapped on his back, stands in hatch of submarine's "doghouse" waiting for the order to embark. Doghouse is so named, navy men say, because in olden days the structure, just behind the conning tower, resembled a doghouse in shape.

A lone Marine provides an early warning source against any enemy infiltration attempt from atop his improvised observation post; the Vietnamese were very adapt in the use of field craft.

LAST MARINE "ADVISOR" REPORT

1975

Lieutenant General Anthony Lukeman

1. General. At the time the withdrawals in MR-I and MR-II were ordered, the Marine Division had approximately 11,000 men in its area of operations in northern MR-I; fully equipped, well trained, well-led and combat tested. Approximately 4,000 of those men disembarked at Vung Tau in MR-III on 2 April. An additional 1,500 or so rejoined their units in the weeks preceding the surrender; most having escaped by small boat, some having walked from the vicinity of Cam Ranh Bay after disembarking there following the withdrawal from Danang. All major equipment and about half of the individual equipment and weapons of the individuals who were able to withdraw and find transport to MR-III were lost. The 147 Brigade, one of the four brigades of the division, lost over 80% of its people as it attempted to withdraw from positions in defense of Hue city. Other units experienced their most serious losses during the withdrawal from Danang, in which most of the Marines who were able to get aboard ships did so, by swimming. Many Marines were drowned in the attempt, the enemy on the beaches killed others, and some (who could not swim) undoubtedly were captured.

2. Military Evaluation of the Marines' Withdrawal. The Vietnamese Marine Commandant, Major General Bui The Lan, discussed the withdrawal with a U.S. Marine officer who worked with Major General Lan and his staff during the preceding ten months. Major General Lan stressed five military aspects of the withdrawal, which, although inseparable from the political aspects, can be described as follows:

    a.   The division was ordered on 23 March to defend at all cost its positions north of Hue city. The positions were held at that time by the 147th Brigade, task organized with four infantry battalions (3rd, 4th, 5th and 7th), one artillery battalion, and various support units. Brigade strength was about 3,000 men. (Other Marine units had previously been redeployed to positions in defense of Danang following the removal of the Airborne Division from that area.) The 147 Brigade was preparing to execute the order to defend when it was ordered to withdraw. Its men had been psychologically prepared to stay and fight. The division was not in contact with the enemy. An adverse effect on morale was inevitable. (In retrospect, the withdrawal was a tactical error: almost total personnel and equipment losses were sustained by the 147 Marine Brigade with no attrition of the enemy force.)

    b.   The rear area during the withdrawal from Hue and later during the operations around Danang was clogged with thousands of armed stragglers from other military units and with scores of thousands of civilians. Tactical movement during the withdrawal was impossible.

    c.   Other MR-I ground units dissolved. Part of national strategy had been to locate most ground forces in their home areas, thereby taking advantage of individuals' motivation to defend their homes and families. When troops from those units were ordered to withdraw, their homes were forfeited and their families became refugees; many troops reverted to being individuals rather than members of military units. They deserted their military units and joined their families as refugees. (The Marine Division troops did not have the same conflicting motivations; most had been recruited in MR-III. As one of two strategic reserve divisions, the Marine Division was operating away from the area where the families of its troops lived.)

    d.   Coordination between air, ground and naval units in MR-I was poor.

    e.   The enemy's tactics were effective: he attacked with rockets and artillery against populated areas then (at Danang) with tanks on three axes lightly supported by infantry. Civilian panic, additional military desertions, and increased difficulty of movement in the rear followed.

3. Supplies And Equipment Lost And Destroyed:

    a.   All of the major equipment, the individual equipment and weapons of troops who were killed or captured, and about half of the individual equipment and weapons of troops who returned were lost.

    b.   The division was able to destroy about 40% of its ammunition on position, 120 of about 200 cargo trucks, and 60 of 60 artillery pieces. All of the division's 15 TOW systems were dumped in the surf, as were most of the crew-served weapons.

    c.   Factors leading to the loss of the remaining equipment and supplies were:

        (1)   The unexpected order to withdraw immediately from the Hue defensive positions, precluding adequate planning. At the time the order was given, positions were being improved and resupplied in preparation for defensive combat.

(2) The physical problem of ships and craft that could not beach or close on a pier or other loading area.

(3) The rapidity of withdrawal.

(4) The complication of a civilian population mixed with thousands of armed stragglers, making movement and order in the beach areas nearly impossible.

4. Action To Restore Combat Effectiveness

a.   The Marine Division was met at Vung Tau by a resupply convoy sent by its rear headquarters in Saigon, containing water, food, medical supplies, and clothing. A second resupply of ammunition, mobile maintenance equipment, and additional clothing and individual equipment arrived two days later.

b.   The division was given first priority for reequipping by the Joint General Staff and started receiving weapons and vehicles at the end of the first week in April.

c.   A brigade of three infantry battalions and one artillery battalion was ready for deployment by 15 April and was committed to defensive positions east of Long Binh.

d.   A second brigade was formed and deployed in the same area approximately ten days later; however, the effectiveness of the second brigade was questionable, with relatively inexperienced company grade officers and many under trained recruits in ranks. (Five battalion commanders and about forty company commanders had been killed in MR-I. Most recruits were reassigned to combat units during the last week of April, many with as little as four weeks of training.)

e.   The division (-) was not in contact during mid-April. By the beginning of the last week of April, both brigades were in the vicinity of Long Binh, and Division headquarters and a force of about one battalion (-) was located at Vung Tau. On 27 or 28 April, the division apparently had received orders to secure part of Route 15 east of Long Binh. No report exists of the division's performance in that mission.

5. Evacuation. C-130 aircraft evacuated 183 Marine dependents, from Vung Tau on 27 April, with precision and total security. An additional 43 dependents were among the last evacuees from the DAO compound on 29 April. No Marine officers or enlisted men were evacuated prior to the surrender. Subsequent to the surrender some Marines, made their way to shipping in the vicinity of Vung Tau including the Commandant, Major General Lan.

Vietnamese Marine Advisors Colloquium, US Naval Academy, Annapolis, MD, 23 February 1972. Capt Ray Smith (left), Maj Don Price (center), and Capt Jack Murray (right) examine a North Vietnamese tank commander's helmet captured during the 1972 Easter Offensive in Quang Tri Province, Vietnam.

They shall grow not old as we that are left grow old. Age shall not weary them nor the years condemn. At the going down of the sun, and in the morning, we will remember them.

When you go home tell them of us and say. For your tomorrow we gave today.

—Taken from the British 2nd Division Memorial at Kohima, Burma

Vietnamese Marine Advisors Colloquium, U.S. Naval Academy Officers Club, Annapolis, MD, 23 February 1973. Front row (left to right) Capt Ray Smith, Maj Walt Boomer, Capt Phil Norton, Capt Tony Hernandez, Maj Bill Warren, Maj Don Price, Capt John Lacy, Capt Lance Zellers, Capt Jack Murray, Capt George Philip. Back row (left to right) Capt Al Nettlingham, Capt Bill Wischmeyer, Capt Jerry McClung, Maj Bob Sheridan, Maj Jon Easley (obscured), Maj Ollie Whipple, Capt Dave Randall, Capt Jim Amendolia, Capt Larry Livingston. Capts Smith and Livingston both awarded Navy Crosses during the 1972 Easter Offensive; Majs Boomer and Price won Silver Stars.

THE MOURNER OF THE MILITARY CEMETERY

Major, M.C. Tran Xuan Dung

Immobile near the Bien Hoa Highway
You sit, your gun across your lap.
The sun's dying rays illuminate but half your face –
Why such melancholy in your eyes?

The statue of a mourner…but who are you?
They came back from all corners of the country;
Was it Binh Gia, with its dark rubber plantations?
Or do your soles bear traces of foggy Kontum's red earth?

Civilians would often catch a fleeting glimpse of your shadow
In the mountains and jungles of Bong Son,
Near the foot of Phu Cu Pass.
There's blood on the sleeve of your faded fatigues.

I come from a poor village,
A village in Gio Linh.
You had come to fight there many a time,
Though your chances of leaving alive were slim.

When you heard the name "Quang Tri"
Your eyes would light up,
Just like when "Dong Ha" and the "Thach Han River" were mentioned
And your gaze would rest in the far off distance as if recalling the charms of a lover.

Who are you? Are you of the Airborne perhaps?
A row of medals glitter on your chest.
In the evening light I suddenly realise
That the light is playing on both the medals and the oozing blood beneath them.

Your combat fatigues seem to be changing:
The camouflage pattern fades to black,
And the insignia on your sleeve metamorphoses
Into that of other Army Corps.

Now you are a "Killer Shark", then you are a "Sea Eagle",
Your forearms bear the words "Death to Communists",
Were you a Marine
Who had fought so valiantly in the summer of '72?

I hold a glass to your lips,
It holds the sweet milk of Tam Quan coconuts.
Why do your press your lips together?
So firmly pressed, and so cold to the touch like steel.

Dusk bids its last adieus, and a shiver traces my spine,
In the last of the light the flag is reflected in your eyes.
You are proud to have died for your country…
But in which battle did you die?

AN EPOCH OF SURVIVAL

Life goes on, even during a war...the impressions and images of the Vietnamese people will remain for a lifetime....

Ears of corn (bap), purchased from a peddler, make a good noon meal. Note the "non la," the famous Vietnamese conical hat.

Kindness and patience with their children is a Vietnamese trait...a young boy (con trai) receives his first haircut.

The tenacity and spirit of the Vietnamese people is reflected in the eyes of this villager. The cross on his chest shows that he is a Catholic (cong giao).

Vietnam is noted for its craftsmen; deft hands and creative minds are characteristic of the Vietnamese.

A child learns at her Mother's side; this young girl (con gai) helps with the cooking.